God's Passion

God's Passion

Praying with Mark

Terry Hinks

DARTON·LONGMAN+TODD

First published in 2011 by
Darton, Longman and Todd Ltd
1 Spencer Court
140–142 Wandsworth High Street
London SW18 4JJ

ISBN: 978-0-232-52838-1

A catalogue record for this book is available from the British Library.

Printed and bound in Great Britain by CPI Antony Rowe,
Chippenham and Eastbourne

Contents

Introduction to the Series: Prayer in the Four Gospels

With the immense changes that society has undergone in recent decades, prayer has become immensely challenging for Christians in the West. The great civil rights activist and Christian preacher Martin Luther King, who died from an assassin's bullet on 4 April 1968, said: 'To be a Christian without prayer is no more possible than to be alive without breathing.'[1] Yet many of us, as twenty-first-century Western Christians, are in a sense asthmatic in our praying, struggling to breathe the life of God in our daily lives. The pressures of the surrounding consumer culture deaden our sense of dependence on God. The scandals of political sleaze and spin and the constant drip of media negativity make us feel unable to trust words. The weaknesses and divisions in the Church undermine our sense of a community of prayer. The reality of many different faiths and world-views, together with the vitriolic debates over the very existence of God, sap our confidence in the One who can repair our hearts. Jesus' parable of God's Word being sown in the soil of human lives speaks to our situation today, with its picture of the difficulties that life-giving seed has to take root: the hardened path and hungry birds, the rocks and scorching sun, the choking thorns and withering roots.

Where can we turn in response to all these manifold challenges? To whom can we call out? The very riches of our Christian tradition can at times add to our confusion rather than leading us through it. We can turn to any number of writers or spiritual guides for advice on prayer and spirituality, from this or any century.

Yet we seek one who speaks with greater clarity, greater authority, greater reality, and for Christians that sends them back to the one they claim to follow: Jesus, the carpenter from Nazareth, the man of Galilee, the Christ, the Son of God. Each of the four gospels found in the New Testament make these great claims and invites us to meet and hear and be touched by this figure from first-century Palestine who still calls people in our century to follow. The earliest gospel reports that the people 'were astounded at his teaching, for he taught them as one having authority, and not as the scribes' (Mark 1:22). The last of the four canonical reflections on the life of Jesus – John's gospel – speaks of Jesus asking the disciples if they to want to turn back from following him, to which Simon Peter replies: 'Lord, to whom can we go? You have the words of eternal life' (John 6:68).

But can this word of authority speak across the centuries to our own time, a time when 'authority' is often seen in terms of oppression, false certainty and delusion? Can it overcome the huge walls of distrust that have developed within our Western hearts?

Jesus' authority was not derived from educational, religious, social or political status. He had no political power and stood outside the religious hierarchy, at the edge of the institution, steeped in his own Jewish tradition and faith but at the same time critical of it. He had the freedom to speak new words and act in surprising ways.

His authority was not an imposed or oppressive one, but one generated by the integrity of his life, the insight of his words and the gift of the Spirit. It was especially recognised by the ordinary people of Palestine – people who had no claims on authority for themselves and so do not feel threatened by Jesus' authority.

In our twenty-first-century Western society we are all our own authorities and so resistant to outside authorities. We want to control 'what is true for us' and ignore uncomfortable challenges to our own self-determination. It is often those moments of vulnerability, when our defences are down and our self-importance threatened, that we are at our most receptive to this authoritative word that comes from beyond us.

I believe that Word which astounded Jesus' listeners can still speak to us – not to oppress us but to liberate us. But we need to be opened (the great *ephphatha* of Mark's gospel). The Spirit, which so filled Jesus and which he promised to his followers, needs to dig over the ground, cutting down the weeds, clearing some of the stones, nourishing the soil of our hearts to receive the Living Word and to bear fruit in our daily lives. Praying with the gospels will be above all about that process of being opened again and again.

Sister Wendy Beckett writes in the introduction to her book of meditations on art, *The Gaze of Love*:

> Books on prayer are dangerous ... At some level that we do not recognise, we may well be reading books on prayer as a way to allay our guilt about not actually praying. The over-weight, it is said, are devoted readers of diet books, the sedentary devour travel books. Reading about prayer, talking about prayer, even writing about prayer: these are not useless activities but they are dangerous.[2]

All too easily, reading books about prayer can become an alternative to praying, and reading books about the gospels an alternative to reading the gospels themselves.

Since the four gospels were written and then later accepted within the canon of Scripture, Christians have tended to conflate them into one general story about Jesus, losing sight of the distinctive voice of each gospel. There is real value in giving each gospel sufficient attention to hear the writer's distinct voice as they bear witness to the events of Jesus' life, death and resurrection and relate that story to their own time and situation.

The early Church Fathers delighted in this fourfold witness and came to link the four gospel-writers to the four living creatures of Ezekiel's vision of heaven (Ezekiel 1:4–10) and described again in the Revelation to John: 'Around the throne, and on each side of the throne, are four living creatures full of eyes in front and behind: the first living creature like a lion, the second living creature like an ox, the third living creature with a face like a human face, and the fourth living creature was like a flying eagle' (Revelation 4:6, 7). Matthew, who began his gospel with the human ancestry of Jesus, came to be signified by the human face. The lion signifies Mark, the voice of the lion roaring in the desert – 'Prepare the way of the Lord.' Luke, who began his gospel with Zechariah, the priest at the altar, is signified by the sacrificial animal, the ox. John, the messenger of the Word, is represented by the soaring eagle.

There is good reason for there to be four gospels within the Christian canon of Scripture rather than simply one. As Stephen Barton points out in his book *The Spirituality of the Gospels*, the four gospels can be 'mutually reinforcing' and 'mutually correcting'.[3] Ultimately there is only one Gospel – the good news of Jesus Christ, announcer of the kingdom, teacher and healer, crucified Saviour and risen Lord. Yet there are four witnesses showing the glorious multifaceted nature of that Gospel, which can speak to Jew and Gentile, rich and poor, male and female. As we pray with the gospels we give thanks for that variety and distinctiveness alongside the underlying oneness.

∞

God of all time,
we rejoice in the company of all your gospel people.
We give thanks for those first eyewitnesses
        who told the story of Jesus
    for the young and growing Christian community
            re-telling the news that had set it alight
    and for those who gathered and wrote down
            the stories of Jesus
            for their own times and communities.

We praise you
        for Matthew the human messenger, who assures us
that Jesus is with us always and will be met in the naked,
the imprisoned and the hungry;
        for Mark, the roaring lion, who roars out to us to turn
round and believe the good news, leads us to the cross and
shows us the Strong One who defeats evil and death itself;
        for Luke, the great ox who speaks of searching and
sacrifice, songs and surprising joy and the new dawn that
Jesus brings;
        and for John, the soaring eagle, who takes us to the
heights of Christ's glory and opens to us life in Christ's
name – life in abundance.

We give thanks
    for those who brought the gospels to our own land
and those who translated them into our own tongue;
    for scholars wrestling with their message and
preachers retelling the Word of life;
    and for those in every generation whose lives have
been changed and challenged by the truth and grace that
flows through these words.

∞

Praying with the gospels is about letting Jesus teach us how to pray, rather than imposing our ideas about prayer on him. The gospels show us how to pray by Jesus' teaching, the way he prayed, his impact on people around him and their response to him. The pinnacle of that teaching is the Lord's Prayer. Michael Mayne described it as 'a kind of signature tune' for all Christians: 'it contains all we will ever need to express our trusting relationship with God and our dependence on him. To say it slowly, in a thankful spirit, is sufficient, even though unwrapping the layers of meaning in the words "our" and "Father" might take a lifetime.'[4]

The Lord's Prayer is given in the liturgical version Christians are familiar with today in Matthew's gospel (Matthew 6:9–13) and in a simpler and perhaps earlier form in Luke's gospel (Luke 11:2–4).

Matthew (Book of Common Prayer)	Matthew (NRSV)	Luke (NRVS)
Our Father which art in heaven hallowed be thy name Thy kingdom come. Thy will be done, in earth as it is in heaven. Give us this day our daily bread. And forgive us our trespasses, as we forgive those who trespass against us. And lead us not into temptation; but deliver us from evil: for thine is the kingdom, the power and the glory, for ever and ever.	Our Father in heaven, hallowed be your name. Your kingdom come. Your will be done, on earth as it is in heaven. Give us this day our daily bread. And forgive us our debts, as we also have forgiven our debtors. And do not bring us to the time of trial, but rescue us from the evil one. (*doxology not included in the oldest manuscripts*)	Father, hallowed be your name. Your kingdom come. Give us each day our daily bread. And forgive us our sins, for we ourselves forgive everyone indebted to us. And do not bring us to the time of trial.

Mark has no record of the Lord's Prayer within his gospel, but the key elements of that prayer are to be found there too, in Jesus' praying 'Father' (the Aramaic 'Abba') in the garden of Gethsemane (14:36); his message about God's kingdom (1:14; 4:11, 26 etc.); his prayer 'not what I want, but what you want' (14:36); his thanksgiving for bread (in the meals of 6:41; 8:6; 14:22), his words about forgiveness – 'whenever you stand praying, forgive, if you have anything against anyone, so that your Father in heaven may also forgive you your trespasses' (11:25) – and words of warning to his disciples – 'Keep awake and pray that you may not come to the time of trial' (14:38). Whether this was because Mark was familiar with the Lord's Prayer or simply with Jesus' teaching which is summed up within it we do not know. It does show, however, the importance given to these key gospel themes of God as caring, compassionate Father, seeking the kingdom, doing God's will, daily dependence on God's provision, forgiveness and forgiving, struggle with challenge and evil. Summed up in the Lord's Prayer, these gospel themes flow through Jesus' teaching on prayer.

Like Mark, John does not record the Lord's Prayer, as he gives more focus to who Jesus is than what he teaches. This christological focus means that the teaching contained within the Prayer is given instead in reflections on the person of Christ. John reflects repeatedly on the closeness – in fact oneness – of the Son and the Father and speaks in his prologue of this relationship being opened up to those who receive 'the Word made flesh': 'But to all who received him, who believed in his name he gave power to become children of God, who were born not of blood or of the will of the flesh but of God' (John 1:13). There are few references to the kingdom of God in John's gospel, the focus having shifted from the kingdom to the King – Jesus Christ. However, as he stands before Pilate, Jesus speaks of the kingdom as being his: 'my kingdom is not from this world' (John 18:36). For John, doing the will of God is about believing in Jesus. The bread is not so much daily provision as the heavenly sacramental food of Jesus: 'I am the bread of life. Whoever comes to me will never be hungry, and whoever believes in me will never be thirsty' (John 6:35). Forgiveness remains an important theme ('God did not send his Son to condemn the world …', John 3:17), and the disciples are sent out to carry that forgiveness to the world: 'if you forgive the sins of any they are forgiven' (John 20:23). The theme is developed in the gospel's reflections on dwelling in the love of Christ: Jesus instructs his disciples, 'love one another as I have loved you' (John 15:12). John, like the other writers, recognises the struggle with persecution and evil but expresses it in more cosmic terms of the battle between light and darkness. His tone is triumphant: 'the light shines in the darkness and the darkness did not overcome it' (John 1:5).

The disciples' request 'Lord teach us to pray' (Luke 11:1) arises from the way Jesus is praying (once again withdrawing with his followers to 'a certain place'). This contrasts with the way Matthew includes the Lord's Prayer within a section on prayer in the great 'Sermon on the Mount' (Matthew 6:5–13). Matthew emphasises Jesus as the teacher or the new lawgiver, sitting down on the mountain to teach his disciples (Matthew 5:1). Luke has placed Jesus' teaching about prayer as following Jesus' action of praying: the reader is encouraged not simply to follow the words of Jesus, but to follow his example: to pray not simply as he taught, but as he prayed.

The request is not simply 'Lord, teach us to pray', but to teach 'as John the Baptist had taught his disciples'. There is a recognition here that the teaching of prayer follows a long tradition: Jesus is asked to teach his followers as John the Baptist had taught his disciples (and as other rabbis had done in the past). Jesus stands within this tradition – and Jesus and the gospel-writers recognise the value of that tradition – but at the same time Jesus brings a new depth and intensity to the reality of prayer.

∞

Reflect and pray

When we do not know how to begin,
   Lord, teach us to pray.
When we are caught up in ourselves and closed to God,
   Lord, teach us to pray.
When we are overwhelmed with our own insignificance,
   Lord, teach us to pray.

When we have prayed and spoken and failed to listen,
  Lord, teach us to pray.
When we have reduced prayer to words and lists and books,
  Lord, teach us to pray.
When we have failed to breathe in the Spirit,
  Lord, teach us to pray.
When we have found prayer to be dull and un-nourishing,
  Lord, teach us to pray.
When we have become comfortable with our way of praying,
  Lord, teach us to pray.
When we cease to sense the grace and wonder of God,
  Lord, teach us to pray.
When we have narrowed prayer to 'me and my God' and
  forgotten our brothers and sisters,
  Lord, teach us to pray.
When we are tempted by pride or despair, complacency or
  cynicism,
  Lord, teach us to pray.
When we have prayed and not acted on our praying,
  Lord, teach us to pray.
When we think we know exactly how to pray,
  Lord, teach us to pray.

∽

In each of the gospels, Gethsemane is the supreme point of prayer, the moment when Jesus wrestles with his own human hopes and fears and then enfolds his will within the greater divine will. This is true even in John's gospel where the event is not recorded but only hinted at. The different ways the four gospels handle this story show both their distinctiveness and the common themes in them all.

In Mark it is where Jesus expresses his real human emotions and then goes on to pray 'Abba, Father', a moment of intensity and intimacy, yet also one where God seems absent and silent. Working from Mark's manuscript, Matthew omits the Aramaic word 'Abba' (as does Luke) but personalises Jesus' address to God as 'My Father', emphasising the three times Jesus prays. He underlines the importance and development of Jesus' praying by placing the prayer in two parts, beginning each with the words 'My Father' and ending them with 'your will be done'. The essence for Matthew is Jesus' seeking after God's will, despite the cost to himself.

For Luke the garden is the point of supreme struggle for Jesus, the final temptation for which the devil has been biding his time (Luke 4:13). In Luke's eyes Jesus' victory and obedience in the garden enable him to pray with confidence on the cross: 'Father forgive them …' (Luke 23:34) and 'Father into your hands I commend my spirit' (Luke 23:46). Luke has no cry of dereliction from the cross ('My God my God why have you forsaken me?', Matthew 27:46 and Mark 15:34), perhaps because that cry was given in the garden: 'in his anguish he prayed more earnestly and his sweat became like great drops of blood' (Luke 22:44), a verse not present in some of the oldest manuscripts but vividly describes Jesus' inner struggle.

John in a sense denies that the struggle takes place at all. The garden is mentioned as a place where Jesus and his disciples go after the supper and as the place where Jesus is arrested, but not as a place of prayer. Instead Jesus prays for his friends before they leave for the garden (John 17). The garden prayer is hinted at in an earlier verse: 'Now my soul is troubled. And what should I say – "Father, save me from this hour"? No, it is for this reason that I have come to this hour. Father, glorify your name' (John 12:27). Here Jesus expresses sorrow, and hints at the struggle in the garden that the other gospels describe, but quickly moves to self-offering and affirmation. It is not that the Jesus of John's gospel cannot feel human emotions; indeed, John gives us a number of deeply moving pictures of Jesus' compassion, such as his weeping at the death of Lazarus (John 11:35, 38). But at this point in his gospel, John passes over the struggle of Gethsemane to affirm Jesus' sense of mission from God, oneness with the Father's loving purpose and desire to glorify God's name through his actions: 'God so loved the world that he sent his Son …' (John 3:16).

Here in the prayer of Gethsemane is prayer at its most intense and real and also most trusting and self-giving. It will shed dazzling light on our praying and expose the ways in which we avoid that intense struggle ('if it is possible, take this cup from me'), that deep intimacy ('Abba, my Father') and that seeking to align with the saving will and purpose of God ('not my will, but yours be done'), despite the personal cost. This is not determinism or stoic submission to some impersonal fate; this is a placing of self-will within a bigger purpose, the refusal to run away from the call of God.

Each gospel helps us to explore prayer in different ways and can stretch our own praying in new directions, but each ultimately brings us back to that picture of Jesus drawing courage to face the cross, to enter the heart of human suffering and to place himself into the hands of the God who is 'Abba' – the One who can be trusted and truly loved – and the God who can do impossible things – even raising the dead to new life.

∞

Reflect and pray

Good News God,
we thank you for the gospel-writers
in all their uniqueness.
We thank you for your Spirit
at work in them and us.
Through their words
speak your Living Word,
point us to the Jesus of history,
the Christ of faith, the risen Lord
who calls us to follow today,
the One who promised to be with us
always to the end of time.
We ask this in his name.

∞

Ways to pray with the gospels

Praying with the gospels is essentially about giving their words and stories a deeper attention, within the context of God's reality and presence. Without that time and attention – that space and silence – we will not be able to allow them to touch us. Christopher Burdon comments:

Accustomed to instant colour pictures our age needs to relearn the patience and imagination simply to listen to stories – not only the parables of Jesus, but the whole parable of Jesus himself, or rather the four parables of Matthew, Mark, Luke and John, that cannot be compressed into a single synopsis or doctrinal scheme.[5]

As well as giving attention to the story, we need to make some conscious acknowledgement of the presence and involvement of God in our praying. Without this, prayer will not happen – we will only be talking to ourselves. In his exploration of prayer in the Old Testament, Walter Brueggemann stresses the quality of dialogue in Israel's prayer, 'in which both parties are free and both parties are at risk', and goes on to write:

Such prayer serves to counter the enormous temptation to monologue that causes a nullification of the human spirit. Monologue is everywhere among us – in absolute theology, absolute patriotism, absolute authority, absolute autonomy – any practice that assures we can live without being decisively impinged upon by 'the other.' In Israel's purview, the neighbour is one who impinges as 'other.' And behind the neighbour stands God, who impinges on life and will be impinged upon by Israel at prayer.[6]

Setting our reading of the gospel stories within the context of prayer compels us to direct our response to the gospel story (be it questions or commitment, joy or doubt) towards God. It encourages us to seek the help of God's Spirit to enlighten and connect the story with our own situation. A dialogue is set up, on the one level between ourselves and the gospel-writer and at a more basic level between our deepest selves and God – the Spirit of God at work within us.

Of course reaching that point of encounter is not without difficulty. Our natural human impatience tends to make us want to hear instant answers, rather than to struggle with words and stories that come from a very different culture and world-view to our own. Our own agendas and prejudices can get in the way of truly listening and responding. Within the gospels Jesus recognises how prayer can be distorted and misused, becoming at times a way of boosting personal ego rather than seeking God. He sees his task as redirecting people to 'the Father who sees in secret' and to true love for God and for neighbour.

Alongside impatience and self-centredness, distractions from outside and within our minds can become barriers to our being still before God, listening openly to the Gospel and speaking to God from the heart. A wise prayer guide reminds us: 'There are two golden rules of prayer. One is that we have to pray as we can in the way best suited to us, not in the way we think we ought … And the other rule is: the less we pray, the harder it gets.'[7]

Christopher Burdon speaks of the need to relearn patience and imagination. These are two essential tools as we approach praying with the gospels. The renewed interest in *lectio divina* has in a sense been a rediscovery of the value of patient waiting and listening, as we absorb the text of Scripture, reading slowly and repeatedly and chewing over its words. Eugene Peterson draws the analogy of eating Scripture and comments:

> Lectio divina is the deliberate and intentional practice of making the transition from the kind of reading that treats and handles, however reverently, Jesus dead, to a way of reading that frequents the company of friends who are listening to, accompanying and following Jesus alive.[8]

Lectio divina involves a fourfold movement of *lectio* (reading the passage slowly and prayerfully), *meditatio* (reflecting on the words that strike one), *oratio* (responding in simple prayer) and *contemplatio* (entering stillness before God, seeing life in that light and absorbing God's love). David Foster reminds us that 'we need to begin lectio in the context of prayer'.[9] That starting point is essential to counteract the personal agendas and prejudices that we inevitably bring to our reading. So he goes on to say: 'Put yourself in the presence of God. Let go of the immediate things on your mind, and turn your heart to the God who dwells within.'[10]

Gabriel O' Donnell rightly emphasises: 'Lectio is a disciplined form of devotion and not a method of Bible study. It is done purely and simply to come to know God and be brought before his Word, to listen.'[11]

It is important that we do not reduce our reading of the gospel or our praying to a technique. All our reading and praying needs a humility and an honesty which is totally at odds with any sense of learning or mastering a method. The Living God is bigger than all our methods and the working of God's Spirit is essential to breathe life into our forms of reading and praying.

If *lectio* reminds us of the need for patience, the Ignatian tradition reminds us of the place of imagination. As we work with the gospels we work with stories, metaphors and word pictures, rather than Mr Gradgrind's 'facts, facts, facts'.[12] In his *Spiritual Exercises*, Ignatius of Loyola encouraged his followers to hear and enter the gospel stories. That act of imagination allowed the stories to speak in a fresh and powerful way, and the Ignatian spiritual exercises continue to do this to this day. As John Pritchard explains: 'we watch the event from inside the story, not from reading pages of a book, and this in turn may bring us face to face with Jesus himself, and our conversation with him can be a most precious encounter and the most personal of prayers.'[13]

Imagination is not about making things up, but about enlarging our seeing. That strange but great eighteenth-century visionary William Blake famously said:

> And I know that This World Is a World of
> IMAGINATION & Vision. I see Every thing I paint In
> This World, but Every body does not see alike. To the
> Eyes of a Miser a Guinea is more beautiful than the Sun,
> & a bag worn with the use of Money has more beautiful
> proportions than a Vine filled with Grapes. The tree
> which moves some to tears of joy is in the Eyes of others
> only a Green thing that stands in the Way.[14]

Imagination is a key tool in prayer. After all, we are relating to a Reality that is beyond our sight and our grasp. Imagination is also a key tool in our reading of the gospels, for if they do not touch our imagination they will remain dry and dusty ancient documents. It is as we relate to the gospel characters, as we become caught up in the story and captivated by its central figure, that Jesus meets and speaks to us in our own times and situations.

However, there is a danger that we impose on the Jesus of the gospels our own assumptions and attitudes. Our imagination can run loose and become detached from the reality of the gospel story or the world in which we live and breathe today. In this we need to recognise our human fallibility, but also our need to rely on the true and living Spirit of God. In our reading and praying of the gospels we are not alone and we do not rely simply on our own resources. We are part of the community of faith, stretching across centuries and continents. More than that, God is nearer than we can possibly imagine, in fact at work by the Spirit at the heart of our being.

∽

Reflect and pray

Come Holy Spirit
enlarge my mind and heart
stretch me in all your ways
to make space for grace
room for the life of Christ
here today. Amen.

∽

The four gospels provide us with the words of Christ and of his followers, words that are 'bigger' than our own. The reciting of set words – the liturgy, the work of the people – has immense value for our individual praying because it connects us with the wider community of faith and reinforces that common faith within our minds and hearts. The very familiarity of the words – as we use them repeatedly – can lead us into a place of greater stillness, where we can sense the Spirit of God moving within us and offer our own prayers from the heart. The interplay of words and silence, familiarity and freshness, communal and personal faith, speaking and listening, is part of the dance of prayer. Of course the recital of familiar words alone can never be sufficient for true prayer to take place: our relationship to God needs to be expressed in a variety of ways, through familiar words and phrases, gestures and actions, spontaneous speech and silent communion.

Reading the Gospel in a context of prayer requires of us to set aside a reasonable amount of time, ideally each day. In our activity-filled lives that setting aside of time may feel very difficult. That difficulty should perhaps alert us to consider how we use and fill our time, and where this 'time filling' has become destructive rather than creative. Finding time and space initially may be very challenging, but patience (in the face of one's failures), persistence (in the face of one's laziness and excuses), and prayer itself (for the Spirit's guiding help) will bear fruit.

For some, early morning will be best, before the business of life takes hold. Martin Luther advised that we should get down to prayer straight away in a morning and ignore 'the deceitful thoughts that keep whispering: wait awhile. In an hour or so I will pray when I finish this or that.'[15] However, clearly for others, work and family activity and demands make the morning a very difficult time to enter into more than a fleeting moment of prayer. Some other time will need to be found, but the essential thing is that we find this space when we can turn off the phone and TV and give God some serious attention. That attention will not be best given if we are either frantic or very sleepy.

The gospels also encourage us to weave prayer into our daily lives, such as by giving thanks for food and other blessings and praying for people we encounter. These prayers can be spoken silently – no more than 'arrow' prayers – but they can shift our perspective on the day and on life. After all the gospels speak of a God not confined to religious times and sacred spaces but involved in the whole of life.

II

A Pattern for Prayer

Introducing a pattern for prayer

I am inviting you to reflect on Mark's gospel over a period of forty days, exploring how forty passages draw us to the One who is made known in Jesus, who came not to be served but to serve and to save us all.

You may wish to use the following pattern for prayer which draws from the four gospels to provide the setting for your reading of Mark. It consists of seven sections but can be used very flexibly. For example, you could use the first three sections – and the last – in the morning and then come back to the other prayers in the evening. You could omit the use of the canticles, psalm-like poems from Luke's gospel, or the written prayers, simply following the headings. You may on different occasions want to focus on thanksgiving, confession or intercession. The pattern is simple enough that it – and some of the key verses – can be memorised and so could be used when walking if that is more helpful. While written for individual use, the pattern could also be used with a prayer partner or small group. It is important that you adapt to your own needs, situation and personality, while not avoiding the real challenge that such gospel praying brings.

The constant pressure on us is to go for a quick fix in prayer and to fail to recognise the patience and persistence required to wait on God and to listen. Quietening our minds and stilling our bodies is an important part of preparing to pray – that going into your own room and shutting the door that Jesus describes in the Sermon on the Mount (Matthew 6:6). But prayer is never simply down to us.

It is not some anxiety-ridden striving after the Invisible, but a conversation with One who knows our needs and our hearts. In Karl Barth's affirming words, 'Prayer is a grace, an offer of God.'[16] Jesus often confronts the disciples' anxieties and again in the Sermon on the Mount tells his disciples not to try to impress God by long prayers: 'your Father knows your needs before you ask him' (Matthew 6:8). Prayer is a meeting of human boldness – the persistence to continue to speak to God, whatever we may feel – and God's grace – the patient loving kindness of God for us all, come what may.

A pattern for prayer

1 Preparing to pray
Enter God's presence in stillness, remembering Jesus beside you and seeking the help of the Spirit within you. Enter the room of God's presence, shutting the door behind you:

Prayer (may be repeated):

Emmanuel – God is with us.

(from Matthew 1:23)

or Blessed be the one who comes in the name of the Lord.

(based on Mark 11:45)

or Glory to God in the highest and peace on earth.

(based on Luke 2:14)

or It is the Spirit that gives life.

(from John 6:63)

2 Seeking God's mercy
Reflect on the ways in which you have distanced yourself from God, drawn back from love for God and neighbour.

Hear, O Israel, the Lord our God, the Lord is one; you shall love
the Lord your God with all your heart, and with all your soul and
with all your mind and with all your strength. And you shall love
your neighbour as yourself.

(Mark 12:29–31)

Prayer (may be repeated):

Lord, have mercy on me, a sinner.

(based on Luke 18:13)

Assurance: Jesus says: 'Friend, your sins are forgiven.'

(based on Luke 5:20)

You may wish to use one of Luke's Canticles of praise:

Morning: The Benedictus (Luke 1:68–79)

Evening: The Magnificat (Luke 1:46b–55)

3 Hearing the Gospel
*Read the gospel passage and reflection; be opened by the Spirit to God's
Word, made known in the story of Jesus*:

The Word became flesh and dwelt among us …
full of grace and truth.

(from John 1:14)

4 Giving thanks and praying for others
Enter a time of prayer:

Father, I thank you ……… (*name causes of thanksgiving*)

Father, forgive ……… (*name people you need to forgive*)

Father, into your hands I commit ……… (*name people and situations in need of God's peace, justice or healing*)

5 Sharing the Abba prayer

Join all Jesus' followers in praying a version of the Lord's Prayer (in words familiar to you or in one of the versions below):

Abba, Father, not what I want, but what you want. Amen.

(Mark 14:36)

or Father, may your name be hallowed.
Your kingdom come.
Give us each day our daily bread
and forgive us our sins,
for we forgive all who have done us wrong;
and do not put us to the test. Amen.

(Luke 11:2–4 REB)

or Our Father in heaven, hallowed be your name,
your kingdom come, your will be done
on earth as it is in heaven.
Give us this day our daily bread.
And forgive us our debts,
as we also have forgiven our debtors.
And do not bring us to the time of trial,
but rescue us from the evil one. Amen.

(Matthew 6:9–13)

or Father, glorify your name. Amen.

(John 12:28a)

You may wish to use another of Luke's canticles:

Canticle: Song of Simeon (Luke 2:29–32)

6 Concluding Prayer

Morning: Lord Jesus,
increase our faith,
renew our love,
deepen our joy,
for the sake of the kingdom.

(based on Luke 17:5)

Evening: Lord Jesus,
             stay with us, we pray, for the day is almost over.
             Send your Spirit to empower our lives
             and to make us true witnesses of your life.

                                      (based on Luke 24:29)

7 *Final reflection*

Reflect on one of the following verses:

Christ came not to be served but to serve
and to give his life for me and for many.
Thanks be to God.

                                      (based on Mark 10:43)

I was lost but now am found; I was dead but now am alive.
Thanks be to God.

                                      (based on Luke 15:32)

Jesus says: 'I am with you always, to the end of time.'
Thanks be to God.

                                      (from Matthew 28:20)

Jesus says: 'Peace be with you. As the Father has sent me,
so I send you.'
Thanks be to God.

                                      (from John 20:21)

Move out of praying, recognising the touch and blessing of God on your life.

III

Introduction to Mark's Gospel

As the first gospel to be written, Mark is a natural place to begin with our exploration of prayer in the gospels. Eugene Peterson notes: 'The Gospel of St Mark is the basic text for Christian spirituality.'[17] However, it is brief and stark in its style and its teaching about prayer is confined to short descriptions of Jesus at prayer and brief sayings about the different dimensions of prayer. There are none of the profound Sermon on the Mount teachings on prayer found in Matthew's gospel, nor the striking parables on prayer in Luke's, nor the great prayers of exaltation and intercession found in John's account.

Yet the brevity of Mark's stories and teaching about prayer should not deceive us into thinking that prayer is unimportant in the gospel narrative. Too many commentators have ignored the theme of prayer in Mark's gospel and for all the many commentaries on it few include prayer within their indexes. In the opening of her dissertation, Sharyn Dowd comments: 'The Markan treatment of prayer has been neglected by scholars. In comparison to Luke, Mark has less material about prayer, and the author is therefore thought to have little interest in prayer.'[18]

However, in reality, prayer is an underlying current throughout the gospel, explicitly referred to at crucial moments and implicit time and again. While Jesus' teaching on prayer is confined largely to one passage (11:22–25), a passage not without difficulty to scholars and preachers alike, Jesus' example of prayer is seen repeatedly. Mark is very clear that discipleship is about following Jesus and this extends to following his way of praying.

The praying of Jesus is bound up with his relationship to God as child to parent. This is highlighted early on with God's affirmation of Jesus as beloved son and the Spirit's empowerment at Jesus' baptism (1:9–11). Then the Spirit drives Jesus into the desert, where Jesus wrestles with temptation during an extended time of spiritual struggle (1:12, 13). As his ministry unfolds he withdraws to a remote place to pray (1:35); he heals by authoritative command (1:25; 5:41) and touch (1:31; 5:27), by words of forgiveness (2:5); he grieves at people's hardness of heart (3:5; 8:12; 9:19); he takes his disciples away to be refreshed (6:31); he has compassion on the crowd (6:34; 8:2); he gives thanks for bread and fish, blessing God before sharing them among the crowds (6:41; 8:6, 7); he goes up the mountain to pray (6:45; also 3:13; 9:2); he looks up to heaven and sighs, before giving the word of healing, 'Ephphatha' (7:34); he blesses children whom the disciples tried to turn away (10:16). Having entered Jerusalem to the crowd's acclamation, he confronts the corruption of the temple, using words of Isaiah, 'My house shall be called a house of prayer'; he sums up the commandments in the great Shema – 'Hear, O Israel' – linking it to love of neighbour; he gives thanks for bread and wine at the Passover meal, his last supper (14:22, 23) and leads his disciples into Gethsemane to pray (14:32–41). The great Abba prayer of Gethsemane then leads onto the desolation of the cross, where Jesus cries out, using words of Psalm 22, 'My God, my God, why have you forsaken me' (15:34). This in turn leads onto the affirmation of the centurion, 'Truly this was God's Son' (15:39), and that of the young man at the tomb, 'Do not be alarmed; you are looking for Jesus of Nazareth, who was crucified. He has been raised; he is not here' (16:6). In these subtle and varied ways prayer flows through the gospel.

If Jesus is the central guide to prayer by his words and example, others within the story also shed light on prayer, positively or negatively. The disciples in particular shed light on the meaning of discipleship by their willingness to follow, but also by their many failures to understand. In her book *In the Company of Jesus*, Elizabeth Struthers Malbon entitles one of the chapters 'The major importance of the Minor Characters in Mark'.[19] Many characters are only referred to once in the gospel story, but each plays a valuable part in outlining what is involved in putting faith in Jesus, responding to him and following him. Some do this positively, such as the widow with her two coins; others do so negatively, such as the rich man who turns away. Yet others give a mixture of failure and insight – such as the father of the sick boy who after initial questions comes to a heartfelt statement of faith.

These minor characters are often people of few words or sometimes no words (such as the woman who anoints Jesus), but their words – and sometimes actions – take a similar form to prayer and no doubt were recognised as such by Mark's early hearers. We hear affirmations directed at Jesus by the crowd: 'he has done everything well' (7:37) and 'Blessed is the one who comes in the name of the Lord' (11:9). Bartimaeus offers a plea for help and pity: 'Jesus, Son of David, have mercy on me!' (10:48), and the father of the sick boy gives a superb prayer of faith: 'I believe; help my unbelief' (9:24).

Many other characters enlighten the gospel's teaching on prayer. The Pharisees do this negatively by their show of long prayers, which do not flow into just actions (12:10), and their demand for signs (8:11). The disciples show both negative and positive responses; they follow Jesus and are taught by him, but also fail to understand and flee when the crisis moment comes. Their sleeping rather than praying in Gethsemane is no doubt recorded to encourage Mark's listeners: prayer is difficult and even the apostles found it so – the flesh is weak – but Jesus continues to encourage all to 'keep awake and pray' (14:38) and gives the Spirit to strengthen us.

Praying to God

Scholars today recognise that Mark is not simply a gatherer of stories about Jesus, arranging them like 'pearls on a string', but a theologian of real worth, ordering his collection of stories with care.[20] Inevitably his picture of God is bound up with the picture of Jesus he gives, but there is no question that God is the key to Jesus' actions and teaching, authority and identity. Jesus does not act on his own initiative or on his own authority; his life and work are bound up with his relationship to his God – of child to parent, Son to Father – and his dependence on the Spirit of God. Mark outlines this in his prologue (1:1–13) in which the pinnacle moment is God's affirmation of Jesus, the voice from heaven, speaking in words echoing Isaiah: 'You are my Son, the Beloved, with whom I am well pleased' (1:11).

The God that is described in the following chapters makes only one other front-of-stage appearance, when on the mountaintop the divine voice from the cloud speaks again, telling Peter, James and John: 'This is my Son, the Beloved: listen to him!' (9:7). However, throughout the gospel, this same God remains the focus of Jesus' teaching, praying and living – and the authority behind his every action.

In terms of prayer, the God whom Jesus proclaims is One that is truly good. He challenges the rich man's glib description of himself as 'good teacher' by saying, 'Why call me good? No one is good but God alone' (10:18). God is to be trusted: again and again Jesus challenges his followers to have faith. 'Have faith in God,' he tells his disciples (11:22) and then goes on to tell them to pray in that faith and that if they do their prayers will be answered.

More than this, 'for God all things are possible' (10:27), a phrase that is repeated at the very point that Jesus faces the cup of suffering and prays: 'Abba Father, for you all things are possible' (14:36). Yet at Gethsemane the goodness of God and the power of God collide. The question of suffering is put in very stark terms as the power and goodness of God meet with the reality of Jesus' suffering (and the suffering of humanity and creation itself). Mark refuses to resolve the tension. It's important, as we explore the phrase 'for God all things are possible', that we recognise that here on the lips of Jesus in Gethsemane it is not a theoretical or philosophical statement, one to be debated in university lecture halls. Rather, it is a heart-rending affirmation of the greatness of God in what we might call in human terms an impossible situation. Following Jewish tradition Jesus and his followers, including the gospel-writer, believed that God had acted in many wondrous ways in history – ways that might be regarded in human terms as impossible. Here is the God who created being out of nothing, light out of darkness, the God who called Moses to lead his people out of slavery, the God who enabled his people to return from exile. In announcing that the elderly Abraham and Sarah are to have a child, God's messenger tells them: 'Is anything too wonderful for God?' (Genesis 18:14). Psalms echoes this theme time and again, praising God for 'awesome deeds' (see Psalms 65:5; 66:3; 106:22; 145:6).

In commenting on Jeremiah's prayer (Jeremiah 32:16–25) and the divine response, 'Is anything too hard for me?', Walter Brueggemann writes: 'There is no doubt that this doxological affirmation of YHWH's capacity to do what the world calls impossible – and Jeremiah's capacity to trust that divine impossibility – continues to echo in the biblical tradition.' He goes on to note how that 'celebration of YHWH's impossibilities ... continues to sound in the faith of the early church in the New Testament.'[21]

Mark's picture of God is One to whom we can be bold to pray, even longing for what seems impossible. Yet we know that suffering is a reality that cannot simply be whitewashed away. The brokenness of the world is deeply set and the task of reordering that world is a hard and costly one. Mark believes that God's power was at work in Jesus and continues to be at work in those who live and act in his name, and that that power can bring amazing new beginnings and deep healing. But he also knows that evil and suffering continue to have real force in the world too.

In one sense God does not do the impossible for Jesus – despite his utter faith in 'Abba' and agonising prayer for the cup to be removed. But then the prayer of Jesus goes further, seeking not so much the removal of the cup as the doing of God's will. The cross becomes that impossible deed of God identifying with the suffering of the world, ransoming and liberating humanity from the deadening power of evil and death. And the cross leads on to that other impossibility that is possible for God – the resurrection of the dead – the heavy stone is moved and Jesus is no longer held in death's grip, 'he has been raised' (16:6).

The One whom Jesus called 'Father'

Characteristic of Jesus' speech about and to God is the word 'Father'. Mark gives surprisingly few references to Jesus' use of this language, but the moments when Jesus does use the term are highly significant ones. The first is as Jesus begins to teach his disciples of the cross that lies ahead of him, a pivotal point in the gospel following Peter's declaration that Jesus is the Messiah. Here Jesus talks of the glory to come: when the Son of Man 'comes in the glory of his Father' (8:39). The secret that Jesus is the Messiah (but one who will suffer) is out. Jesus can speak more openly of his relationship to the Father, though still speaking in the third person, using that fascinating and puzzling term, 'the Son of Man'.

When they are in Jerusalem Jesus speaks of the importance of prayer amid the challenges ahead for the disciples. As he links prayer with forgiveness he speaks of the Father as not his alone but theirs too, commanding them to forgive as they pray, 'so that your Father in heaven may also forgive you your trespasses' (11:26).

Supremely Mark reports Jesus using the Aramaic word 'Abba' as he prays in the garden of Gethsemane. The apostle Paul retains memory of the same word in Romans 8:15 and Galatians 4:6. There has been a huge amount of study of Jesus' use of this word. It is striking in its intimacy and simplicity. Geza Vermes follows James Barr and others in underlining that this is not baby language ('Abba isn't Daddy!') but an 'invocation in which reverence and intimacy are mingled'.[22] Yet it was not a term unique to Jesus. It has its roots in the Hebrew prophets – the image of God as Father to son, or child Israel, is used for example in the book of Hosea: 'When Israel was a child, I loved him and out of Egypt I called my son … I was to them like those who lift infants to their cheeks' (from Hosea 11:1–11). The Psalms speak of God as 'father to the fatherless' (Psalm 68:5) and 'as a father has compassion for his children, so the Lord has compassion toward those who fear him' (Psalm 103:13).

Jesus' use of the word Abba to address God has parallels in the teaching of rabbis at his time and before. There is a story from a century before Christ about Rabbi Hanan, grandson of Honi. When the world was in need of rain the rabbis used to send schoolchildren to Hanan who tugged at his cloak and said, 'Abba, Abba, give us rain.' He prayed to God, 'Lord of the universe, render a service to those who cannot distinguish between the Abba who gives rain and the abba who does not.'[23]

It is clear that Jesus prayed as a first-century Jew influenced by the traditions, language and culture of his time, and the word that he used to speak of, and to, God was influenced by that context. Yet the relationship that that simple word 'Abba' describes is one that reaches beyond time and culture. This is not patriarchal language but relational language. Above all, it draws from the Jewish belief in the sacred covenant – that mutually committed relationship of God to God's people and God's people to God. Jesus summarises, personalises and renews that relationship in addressing the mystery of God as 'Abba'.

In recent decades many Western Christians have begun to question the Church's overemphasis on the fatherhood of God, seeing the language as exclusive, male, hierarchical and limiting. Much has been done to recover other images and in particular feminine images of God within the Scriptures and later spiritual writers. More than this, many have repeated the long-held recognition that all language is inadequate in relation to the one we call 'God'. Mark underlies this sense of mystery in relation to God by using the image of the cloud, hiding the speaker of the divine promise at Jesus' baptism and transfiguration. As Stephen Barton writes, 'In Mark we are struck by the hiddenness of God.'[24]

To pray 'Abba' is not to create our own image of a male fatherly God but to identify with Jesus in the relationship he experienced and lived out. We have to see, and use, the word in the blazing light of Jesus' own words and actions. The God of Jesus is not the God of the philosophers – the unnamed unnameable one, but the God of the covenant – the I AM WHO I AM, the one who acted in history in liberation and rescue. The one whom Jesus called 'Father' is revealed supremely not as Father, but in the face of Jesus. The words from the cloud of mystery point us to the child – God's Son, the Beloved – and call us to listen to him (1:10; 9:7), to be part of his family by seeking and doing God's will (3:35), to become children so as to enter the kingdom (10:15), and to see in the cross the very heart of God (15:39). In the language of Martin Buber, it is to move from an 'I–it/him' relationship to God (however powerful we may feel that it/he to be) to an unconditional 'I–thou' relationship.[25]

Prayer, the cross and the resurrection

Stephen Barton observes that 'Markan spirituality is a dark strenuous spirituality. It is a Gospel of the Passion from beginning to end.'[26] There is certainly an important truth in this statement. The cross is a recurring theme, and a key picture of discipleship is following in that way. Ernest Best writes: 'The death of Jesus broods over the entire Gospel.'[27] On three occasions Jesus tells his disciples of the rejection that faces him in Jerusalem (8:31–38; 9:30–32; 10:32–34) and rebukes Peter for not accepting this reality. He goes on to contrast the human way of thinking with the divine way (8:33). This becomes the driving force of the rest of the gospel, leading up to the entry into Jerusalem and the extended story of Jesus' rejection and passion. The pace of the gospel, so rapid in the first chapters, with their repeated use of *enthus* (immediately) slows to a day-by-day, hour-by-hour timescale as the focus turns from what Jesus does to what is done to him. From his arrest in the garden he becomes the object rather than the subject of the story's action. Vanstone in his great classic *The Stature of Waiting* writes: 'Jesus is still seen as the focus and centre of the story, but now, His centrality is not of the subject of activity and the initiator of events. It is that of the object of activity, of one by whom actions are received, of the one upon whom events bear.' He goes on: 'Jesus is no longer the one who does – He becomes the one who is done to.'[28]

After the first passion prediction, Jesus tells his disciples that they too must take up their cross – either spiritually in self-giving love or literally in the persecution the community faces: 'If anyone wants to become my follower, let them deny themselves and take up the cross and follow me' (8:34).

In fact, each of the three passion predictions is followed by a call to discipleship in this new way of self-giving love. The second is followed by the story of the disciples arguing about who is the greatest, to which Jesus responds: 'Whoever wants to be first must be last of all and servant of all' (9:35), illustrating this with his welcome of a child. The final prediction leads on to the story of John and James requesting the best seats in heaven and Jesus telling all the disciples: 'Whoever wants to be great among you must be your servant ... for the Son of Man came not to be served but to serve and give his life as a ransom for many' (10:35). Mark uses these stories of the self-centred stupidity of the apostles to teach his own community the great lesson of the cross – self-forgetting loving service – as Jesus' pattern to be followed.

The passion focus of Mark's gospel is real – perhaps reflecting the deadly persecution that Mark's community is facing or expecting to face. Prayer is a key tool for building and sustaining a faith within the community that is resilient and fruitful. In Gethsemane Jesus prays and challenges his disciples to pray: 'Keep watch and pray that you may not come into the time of trial ...' (14:38).

Stephen Barton notes that joy is a word that is largely absent from Mark, unlike Luke's gospel where joy is a recurring theme in people's response to the Jesus event.[29] Mark's one reference to joy (*chara*) is in fact a largely negative one. It comes in the interpretation of the rocky ground in the parable of the sower: 'when they hear the word, they receive it with joy. But they have no root, and endure only for a while; then when trouble or persecution arises on account of the word, immediately they fall away' (4:16, 17). Mark appears here to be suspicious of a joyful response that may be shallow; again a response to the challenges his own community is facing.

However, while the focus of Mark is on a resilient and strenuous faith, it is not without the theme of wonder, as people react to the mighty acts of God – in Jesus – with awe and fear. In his study on *The Motif of Wonder in the Gospel of Mark*, Timothy Dwyer identifies thirty-two places in the gospel where the reaction of wonder occurs and then explores these moments of awe in the first and second parts of the gospel, with the story of the transfiguration as the midpoint. He concludes by commenting:

> The evangelist heightens in the story the degree to which those involved were meeting awesome power beyond human categories and understanding. The possibility of the impossible, the unknown and uncontrollable is met. As such the gospel of Mark has a powerful drama and impact.[30]

This sense of wonder and awe that flows through the gospel has negative and positive aspects. It leads some into confusion and bewilderment, while others to a holy fear – in the Hebrew sense of awe before the divine – and worship. It informs Mark's view of prayer and challenges our own as we pray with the gospel.

Also contrary to Stephen Barton's view, the focus is not simply the death of Christ: the cross and resurrection is one saving event in Mark's eyes, and Jesus' three passion predictions all contain the promise of Jesus' rising alongside the expectation of rejection. Mark's theology of fear and wonder influences his resurrection account, where the women tremble in terror and amazement at what God has done. As John Donahue comments: 'These reactions of wonder and surprise accompany the revelation of God in Jesus, and they signify the power of this revelation to unsettle and change human existence.'[31]

For Mark the cross and resurrection are inseparable, the one flowing from the other and completing the other, both part of God's victory over evil and liberation of humanity. Yet they are not simply a past event; they are a pattern for the life of Jesus' followers in their own times. Jesus' call to 'take up the cross and follow me' is a challenge for every generation, a challenge to escape the bonds of self-centredness and follow the risen Christ in self-giving love. This change of focus is encouraged by the act of praying. As Eugene Peterson comments: 'Prayer is the way we work our way out of the comfortable but cramped world of self into the self-denying but spacious world of God.'[32]

Grounding prayer in reality

Gloriously impossible things happen in the gospel that cause wonder and astonishment and lead people to sense God at work. However, on a more fundamental level, the gospel is strongly grounded in material reality. Physicality is an essential element of the story and of prayer within the story. This is an important antidote to those Gnostic tendencies that can see prayer as an escape from physical reality into some purer spiritual realm. Mark – and the Jesus he proclaims – have no such desire to escape, but rather to bring God's kingdom to fruition within the whole of human existence, body, mind and spirit.

There is an important physicality in the gospel – in the camel-hair clothes and leather belt of John the Baptist, the honey and locusts he eats (1:6); the water in which Jesus is drenched (1:10); the fishermen's broken nets (1:19); the food that is eaten (1:29; 2:15); the roof that is broken open (2:4); the old and new cloth (2:27); the seed that grows (4:8); the child's hand that is held (5:41); the green grass (6:39); the loaves and fishes (6:41); the saliva (7:33; 8:23); the cloud (9:7); the cup of water (9:41); the salt (9:50); the donkey, cloaks and leafy branches (11:8); the coins (12:15; 12:42); the ointment of nard (14:3); the crown of thorns (15:16); the torn curtain (15:38); the sunrise (16:2) and very large stone (16:4). Many of these physical objects have some symbolic connotations, but the physicality remains to underline the incarnational worldly reality of Mark's good news.

Prayer requires us to take seriously our body, as well as our mind and spirit. What we do with our body in prayer is significant: standing to pray (11:25) or throwing ourselves on the ground (14:35) will express different emotions and different ways of relating to God.

Where we pray is significant too: the outward appearance prayers of the scribes (12:40) contrast with Jesus' withdrawal to remote places (1:35; 6:46). The great temple of Jerusalem is meant to be 'the House of Prayer for all nations' (11:17) but in Jesus' experience becomes the place of controversy and conflict. Instead, an upper room – with friends gathered in secret – becomes the place where the great prayer of thanksgiving is offered and a garden the place where Jesus' supreme prayer of self-offering is uttered.

The value of place also connects with what we pray for. Jesus, following Jewish tradition, blesses God for the gifts of creation: bread and fish and wine. Physical reality and sustenance are worthy of thanksgiving. Thanksgiving is a key element of Jesus' praying and one we need to relearn in our own times. As Neville Ward noted in his classic book on prayer: 'It is important for understanding the Christian way of life to cultivate the faculty of gratitude and nourish it as much as one can.'[33] He goes on to say that

Christianity wants all people to 'be happy, to be able to live thankfully instead of resentfully'.[34]

Nor is Jesus unafraid to pray for physical healing, a challenge to our sharp separation of 'the physical' and 'the spiritual'. The gospel is full of physical healings, as health, strength, vision, speech, hearing and life itself are restored. These are signs of God's kingdom breaking into reality. The wholeness God desires for his children is brought into being, through Jesus' words and touch and the faith of those who put their trust in him. Yet often in the gospel the physical restoration also speaks of a spiritual reality, experienced as forgiveness, acceptance and love.

Inevitably our praying will be influenced both by the amazing developments of modern science and by the pervading materialism and individualism of our Western world, but reconnecting to physical reality in thanksgiving and petition will be an important part of Mark's lesson on prayer.

Prayer and the Spirit

Within the gospel there is considerable referencing beyond itself – to events and realities not described within the narrative. There is a sense in which Mark does not want his writing to become a substitute for the One to whom it witnesses: the God who is the lead character, though hidden in mystery and wonder; Jesus, the means by which that lead character speaks and acts, both within the written story and among Mark's hearers and readers; and the Holy Spirit, which is one of the key promises of the good news Mark is telling.

Mark's prologue has the Holy Spirit as the great gift that Jesus brings. In describing Jesus, John the Baptist says: 'The one who is more powerful than I is coming after me ... I have baptised you with water; but he will baptise you with the Holy Spirit' (1:8). Yet this general baptism in the Spirit is not described by Mark; it is an event, or series of events, that comes beyond the gospel. Instead, Mark points to it by describing the Spirit's work within Jesus himself and by Jesus' promises for the future.

The Spirit descends on Jesus like a dove, a sign of blessing and peace, as heaven is torn open and Jesus is affirmed as God's Son, God's Beloved, God's Pleasing One (1:10, 11). The Spirit is shown to be the key to that relationship of child to parent, beloved Son to Abba Father, which is at the heart of Jesus' praying and living. Whether Mark knows Paul's letter to the Romans or not, there are echoes here of Paul's description of the Spirit: 'For all who are led by the Spirit are children of God ...' (Romans 8:14–16).

The Spirit is the enabler of that relationship – the 'Go between God' in the well-known phrase of John V. Taylor.[35] That Holy Spirit does not of course simply appear at Jesus' baptism. The Spirit has been at work since the beginning of creation, at odds with the forces of chaos and destruction (and present before the beginning in the eternal life of the Godhead). It is the inspirer of the prophets and writers of Scripture. In the temple debates, Jesus tells his listeners how 'David himself, by the Holy Spirit, declared, "The Lord said to my Lord ..." '(12:36), a quotation from Psalm 110. Mark assumes that his hearers have a good knowledge of the Hebrew Scriptures and wants to underline their Spirit-filled quality.

The Spirit descends on Jesus at his baptism and then drives him out into the wilderness to confront the destructive powers, focused in the tempter Satan. That struggle with evil remains a key note within Jesus' ministry and while there are few direct references to the Spirit it is clear that Mark sees all of Jesus' actions as Spirit empowered. King Herod wonders who Jesus is and why 'these powers are at work in him' (6:14). The great blasphemy that Jesus accuses the scribes of uttering in reaction to the driving out of unclean spirits is not blasphemy against Jesus himself, but against the Spirit by which he lives and works (3:21–29). Calling that Holy Spirit an unclean spirit is calling goodness evil and God Satan, a total inversion of moral truth and as such spiritually fatal (3:28, 29).

The final reference to the work of the Spirit comes as a promise for the future – to the first followers of Jesus and to Mark's own community. Jesus tells his friends of persecutions to come and then instructs them: 'When they bring you to trial and hand you over, do not worry beforehand about what you are to say; but say whatever is given to you at the time, for it is not you who speak, but the Holy Spirit' (13:11). It is a stunning call for faith; trust not only in God and Jesus, but in the Holy Spirit – God at work within the disciples' hearts and minds, giving them the words to say and the courage to speak. That witness in the face of persecution and danger may be in words – as Jesus speaks before the Council – or in silence – as Jesus stands before Pilate – but the sense of reliance on the Spirit flows through both.

While that reference (13:11) is to witnessing to the faith, it could also relate to the Spirit's help in prayer. Mark gives no direct mention of Jesus 'praying in the Spirit' or 'praying in tongues', but there may be an echo of this idea in Jesus' sighs in response to people's hardness of heart and in preparation for an act of healing. Mark alone among the gospel-writers speaks of Jesus sighing in preparation for the healing of the man who is deaf and speech impaired: 'Then looking up to heaven, he sighed and said "Eph-phatha", that is, "Be opened" ' (7:34). Again in response to the Pharisee's demand for a sign from heaven, 'he sighed deeply in his spirit' (18:12). The word *stenazō* (sigh) has the same root as that used by Paul in his letter to the Romans: 'That very Spirit intercedes with sighs too deep for words' (Romans 8:26). It becomes clear that for Mark baptism in the Spirit is an essential part of our praying. That baptism may come in dramatic ways, like the breaking open of heaven, or gentle gradual ways, like the flight of a dove, and perhaps will even go unrecognised apart from its fruits. Yet it will empower our praying, deepen our compassion for others and enable us to pray to God as beloved children.

There is a final reference to the spirit in Mark, during Jesus' great prayer in Gethsemane. In response to his disciples' inability to stay awake and pray, Jesus tells them: 'Keep awake and pray that you may not come to the time of trial; the spirit indeed is willing, but the flesh is weak' (14:38).

In this case the spirit refers to the human spirit rather than the Holy Spirit, but the two are connected. In his commentary on this passage, Joel Marcus emphasises that the contrast between flesh and spirit is not of the classical world's dualism of body and soul, but rather a Jewish contrast between that dimension of human beings which is easily led into sin and opposition to God and that dimension which is capable of overcoming this inclination and acting according to God's will. It is important to understand this, to avoid developing a distorted view of the physical and material world. Marcus goes on to comment: 'It is doubtful moreover, whether Mark's Christian readers could have heard the sentence "The spirit is willing but the flesh is weak" without thinking of their continuing battle with "the flesh" and support by the Holy Spirit (c f Gal 5:17).'[36] The phrase has now become such a hackneyed part of the English language, brought out as reason for inaction, that we perhaps miss that underlying call to rely more on God's Spirit and less on self.

Prayer and the conflict with evil

As Elizabeth Struthers Malbon comments, 'Conflict is the key to the Markan plot.'[37] There is a spiritual battle going on from the very first pages of the gospel and that battle takes many forms. At its most basic it is the conflict of good and evil, God and the devil, Jesus and Satan, which begins in the wilderness and culminates at the cross and empty tomb. Yet the caricatures we tend to have developed to describe 'the devil' do not do justice to the subtlety and depth of this conflict. Evil takes many guises and works in many different ways, hardening hearts and closing minds, corrupting institutions and twisting belief systems. One of the great images of the gospel is of Jesus as the thief breaking into the world and tying up 'the strong man' so that he can liberate humanity (3:27). It is not a literal story but a mythological picture that describes the essence of what Jesus is doing through his ministry, his death and his victory over death.

Of course, all pictures have their limitations and the picture of discipleship as a spiritual battle has its limitations too. For many of us today warfare language has been deeply tainted by the holy wars of the past, the global destruction of war in the twentieth century and the continuing weary conflicts and acts of terrorism of our own times. The old triumphalism of 'Onward Christian Soldiers' can leave a bitter taste in our mouths, as can the hate-filled ranting of some present-day religious extremists.

Yet we cannot avoid the reality of conflict within human experience; Mark recognises the tragedy of that conflict within families and nations (in chapter 13, in particular) and explores how Christians should respond to it. He encourages his listeners to rely on the Spirit (13:11), learn to forgive (11:25), to love neighbour (12:31) and remain loyal to their Lord (8:38). Ched Myers explores the image of the binding of the strong man and notes 'the modern tendency to flee from an increasingly uncertain conflict-ridden history to the refuge of self-absorption or what Christopher Larch termed as the "culture of narcissism" '.[38] He goes on to speak of prayer as a way of learning faith:

> To pray is to believe in a transformation of self and world which seems empirically as impossible as is 'moving mountains' (11:23). What is unbelief but the despair, dictated by dominant powers, that nothing can *really* change, a despair that renders revolutionary vision and practice impotent.[39]

The evil Jesus speaks of in Mark's gospel is not a reality 'out there', but a twisting of our own human hearts and relationships. People are not defiled by food or unclean hands, by ethnicity or gender, but by an inner distortion that requires a healing and restoration, that begins with forgiveness and works out in discipleship. Prayer is a key tool in this work of transformation – in ourselves and the world around us – as Mark makes clear at the end of the story about the healing of the boy with the spirit (9:14–29). The demons or unclean spirits that are very much part of the gospel's way of viewing the world need reinterpreting in our own times and situation. As Morna Hooker points out: 'We no longer think, as Mark and his contemporaries did, of a world dominated by demons.'[40] However, those unclean spirits in the gospel narrative can speak of that inner distortion and captivity that is part of our modern-day experience and of the work of evil in our world. Transformation is both necessary and possible, and the disciples are reminded that prayer is vital in this, as Jesus ends by telling them: 'This kind can come out only by prayer' (9:29).

Prayer and action

Prayer is in essence an expression of love – love for God and love for neighbour (as we bring others into our minds and before God). Iris Murdoch describes prayer as 'simply an attention to God which is a form of love'.[41] Without that motivation of love, prayer becomes superstition based on fear or magic. Asked which was the greatest commandment, Jesus drew on his roots as he quoted the great Shema prayer with which he no doubt began each day and ended each day, following the instructions of Deuteronomy: 'Hear, O Israel: the Lord our God, the Lord is one; you shall love the Lord your God with all your heart and with all your soul and with all your mind and with all your strength' (12:29, 30). Love involves the totality of heart and mind, spirit and will.

True prayer is not simply a mental exercise, but neither is it simply a matter of the heart leaving our mental abilities safely locked away. It is an act of will, strength, as well as a response of our spirits to the touch of God's Spirit. It involves our whole being and fundamentally our being in relationship. Jesus then binds this love of God with love of neighbour, drawing from another book of the Torah with his words, 'You shall love your neighbour as yourself' (Leviticus 19:18).

In Mark's gospel Jesus is insistent that a good faith leads to good fruit – loving action – and is at the same time immensely critical of religious practices that are not matched by just and compassionate deeds. He has harsh words for those who do not connect love for God with love for neighbour. He grieves over the hardness of heart of those who condemn his healing on the Sabbath, telling them: 'Is it lawful to do good or to do harm on the Sabbath, to save life or to kill?' (3:4). He exposes traditions that undermine the care of elderly parents (7:11–12) and questions outward customs that do not change actions (7:14–23). He commends acts of kindness and generosity (9:41; 12:44; 14:6) and condemns scribes who 'devour widows' houses' while offering long prayers to appear especially holy (12:40).

He also stresses that prayer requires a forgiving heart: a right relationship with God is bound up with right relationships with those around us. While speaking about prayer, he tells his disciples:

'Whenever you stand praying, forgive, if you have anything against anyone, so that your Father in heaven may also forgive you your trespasses' (11:25). Prayer that does not bear fruit in our own attitudes and actions is not the praying that Jesus teaches in Mark's gospel.

Prayer and the temple

The temple of Jerusalem was a well-known wonder of the ancient world and regarded with reverence by Jesus and his followers. Ed Sanders writes: 'It is almost impossible to make too much of the Temple in first-century Palestine.'[42] Its destruction by the besieging Roman force sent shockwaves through the dispersed Jewish community, including the growing Christian community with its mixed Jewish and Gentile constituency and its deep Jewish roots. One Jewish teacher of the time said:

> From the day on which the temple was destroyed, the gates of prayer have been closed, as it says, 'Yea when I cry and call for help, He shutteth out my prayer' (Lam 3:8) … but though the gates of prayer are closed, the gates of weeping are not closed, as it says 'hear my prayer O Lord and give ear unto my cry; keep not silence at my tears.'[43]

Mark wrote his gospel around the time of the temple's destruction, possibly a few years before it happened or possibly prompted by it. He drew on Jesus' own ambiguous relationship to the temple to speak of a new way of praying and a new temple. The key verse is Jesus' quotation of Isaiah's vision of the temple as 'a house of prayer for all nations' (11:17). Corrupted by the narrowing of Israel's mission, the exclusion of the Gentiles and the exploitation of the poor, the old temple had, in the eyes of the Marcan Jesus, become a barren fig tree (11:20), a den of robbers (11:17). When the disciples admire the large stones of the temple, Jesus tells them they will all be thrown down (13:2). The destruction of the temple is a sacrilege (13:14), just as is the death of God's Son (14:20), yet both mysteriously are part of God's work of judging and saving the world.

A new, resurrected temple is to be formed not made from stones but focused in the person of Jesus and the community that forms in his name, Jew and Gentile alike, a 'house of prayer for all nations'. The destruction of Jesus on the cross and the destruction of the old temple buildings become intertwined. Yet ironically it is the new temple that experiences destruction first. Peter Walker comments: 'At the time of the crucifixion it seems clear that Jesus is wrong: the new Temple, not the old, is on the point of being destroyed, and the bystanders mock the one who promised "to destroy the Temple" (15:29).'[44] At precisely this moment in Mark's narrative, however, we are taken from the hill of Golgotha to the opposite hill, the Temple Mount, to witness a mysterious event: 'the curtain of the Temple was torn in two from top to bottom' (15:38). As Christopher Burdon comments, 'The sanctuary of God's exclusive presence is laid open.'[45] The Shekhinah (the Divine Presence) breaks out of the temple, leaving it an empty shell, at the very point when Jesus dies and the Roman centurion acclaims him Son of God, echoing the tearing of the heavens and descent of the Spirit at Jesus' baptism. The baptism of death leads on to the raising up of Easter Day, the stone rolled back and Jesus free to walk before his followers to Galilee and beyond.

The symbolism may seem strange and obtuse to our twenty-first-century ears, but the power of this symbolism to Mark's original hearers cannot be underestimated. Here, Mark is saying, is a new focus to your prayers, no longer the temple of Jerusalem, but the person of Jesus raised up and going before you. Prayer no longer is to be directed to Jerusalem or to a temple made with human hands, but to the risen presence of Christ, with his followers in all places. That sense of community in prayer is crucial. As Ernest Best emphasises: 'For Mark the disciple is not a solitary individual but the member of a community.'[46] That new community is to be a house of prayer for all nations, taking up the call of Isaiah to be a light for all peoples.

For all the pressures of persecution on Mark's community he refuses to allow the Church to become a ghetto only interested in

its own; its prayer must always be big – focused on the will of God
for all, the kingdom of God in the world.

∞

God of overwhelming grace,
should the day come when temples and churches
    have crumbled to dust
and grass grows where tower and steeple,
    dome and minaret once stood so proud,
may your generous life-giving Spirit continue its work
    that Spirit we learn from stories of seeds and vineyards
        and children;
    that Spirit we glimpse in the widow
        giving her last two tiny coins
    and the woman breaking open the jar
        of costly perfume;
    that Spirit we see poured out in Jesus,
        hanging on a cross.
Should the wealth of nations rust away
and human knowledge reach its bounds,
may your generous life-giving Spirit continue its work,
finding receptive hearts and minds
and willing hands.
We ask this humbly in the name of the servant Lord,
    Jesus Christ.

IV

Forty Reflections

The forty reflections and prayers offered in this volume are there to encourage you as you pray with Mark's gospel in your own particular situation and with your own perspective. They are of secondary importance compared to the gospel passages them-selves; it is the text that is the key. I hope that working and praying with one passage each day over a period of forty days will enable you to enter Mark's gospel in a new and creative way.

1 Are we ready?

Read Mark 1:1–13.

> *The beginning of the good news of Jesus Christ, the Son of God. (Mark 1:1)*

Mark begins not with a genealogy or the story of Jesus' birth, but by simply stating that, first, this is 'the beginning', second, that this is 'good news', and, third, this good news is 'of Jesus Christ'. The word 'beginning' echoes the book of Genesis, 'In the beginning when God created the heavens and the earth' (Genesis 1:1), and so hints at a new act of creation. The 'good news' is a word that in the Roman Empire was associated with the triumph of emperors and generals in conquering territory and defeating enemies. Mark believes that his story is a story of triumph, though not through political scheming or military might. This is God's upside-down triumph through grace, service and sacrifice. Through Jesus the territory of evil has been broken into, the captives have been freed and death has been overcome. This good news echoes the good news of Isaiah, the prophet named in the next verse, and whose words and images reverberate throughout the gospel. This gospel is the Gospel of Jesus Christ, both in terms of being about Jesus Christ, for he is the content, and belonging to Jesus Christ, for he is the author, on God's behalf.

Mark does not name himself. The title 'according to Mark' was added later and the author himself prefers to be anonymous.[47] We will keep with tradition by referring to the author as Mark, but only as convention. Trying to discover more about the author – or pursuing traditions of the writer being John Mark the companion of Paul or a note-keeper for Peter – is not only useless but contrary to the writer's intention. He wishes to be like the unnamed woman who anointed Jesus with oil: he wants to direct attention to the content and bringer of good news – Jesus Christ.

Get ready to pray

Are we ready, God of grace, for your good news?
Are we ready in heart and mind and spirit?
Are we ready to hear that wilderness voice, preparing the
    way, calling us to turn round and start again?

Are we ready to welcome the One who is so full
    of your Spirit, so immersed in your love?
Are we ready to join that struggle to overcome all
    that distorts and damages and destroys?
Are we ready for that outburst of your gracious power,
that Spirit's song, to echo in our hearts
    and open up our lives?

God of grace, as we journey into this gospel,
    this strange good news –
which is life and death and life renewed,
make us ready and willing to hear and to receive,
to turn and to follow,
that we too may be part of your gospel story
now in this time, this moment. Amen.

2 Call

Read Mark 1:14–34.

And Jesus said to them, 'Follow me.' (Mark 1:17)

This collection of stories leads us from the shore of the Sea of Galilee, via the synagogue at Capernaum, to Simon's house. Each is a significant location for Jesus to show his authority through calling, teaching, exorcism and healing. First Jesus issues his call to follow and to join him in fishing for people – drawing others into the net of grace. The initiative is wholly Jesus'. He sees Simon and Andrew (and then John and James); he speaks; he calls them: 'Follow me and I will make you fish for people' (1:17). The word has its effect and they immediately leave their nets and follow. Mark's repeated use of 'immediately' (*enthus*) propels the narrative forward. The fishing begins at once after the call; there is no preparation period for the disciples, no rabbinical school to train in. Instead the disciples will learn what this work of fishing is about as they follow Jesus.

They will learn rapidly that it is directed at the maimed of life. The scene shifts from shore to synagogue, where the good order and religious propriety of the sacred place of worship is disturbed by a man gripped by 'an unclean spirit' crying out in recognition of who Jesus is. The dehumanising spirit is rebuked, silenced and driven out, leaving those watching amazed.

Hidden within this passage is another call that is often dismissed as no more than a minor domestic incident. Simon's mother-in-law lies sick with a fever and he and his brother Andrew, together with James and John, immediately tell Jesus about her. Here, set between the public acclamation and excitement surrounding Jesus in the synagogue and town, is a personal encounter that brings healing and a glimpse of what the servant ministry of Jesus is about. 'He came and took her by the hand and lifted her up. Then the fever left her, and she began to serve them' (1:31). It is the first of four times when Jesus takes a person by the hand to help them up or to guide them to one side. (The others are the girl at death's door in 5:41, the man who was blind in 8:23 and the boy with convulsions in 9:27.) Each time the picture is an immensely human and tender one that expresses Jesus' care for the individual. The healing is followed by response: the unnamed woman, simply known as Simon's mother-in- law, begins to serve them. Feminist scholars are understandably suspicious of the patriarchal assumptions underlying the story; the woman is not known by her name but by her relation to Simon, and the domestic service she then offers seems to reflect the society of the time where women were expected to serve. However, later in the gospel Jesus tells the disciples that he has come not to be served but to serve, using the same word *diakonei* that is applied to Simon's mother-in-law's service offered to Jesus and the disciples.[48] It seems that even at this early stage in the gospel Mark wants to point out that discipleship is not about male self-aggrandisement but about following Jesus in the way of self-giving. Fred Pratt Green writes in his hymn 'The Church of Christ' that Christ alone 'can cure the fever in our blood and teach us how to share our bread'.[49]

Reflect and pray

Lord Jesus,
friend of fishermen and ordinary folk,
we thank you that you come and interrupt our
    self-contained lives.
You move us with your call,
challenging us to follow your steps and to join your fishing
    expedition.

Lord Jesus,
friend of all,
we thank you that you come into the midst of life,
the workplace with its demands and compromises,
the place of worship and reflection,
the place of sickness and desperate need,
the place of food shared and friendships deepened.

Lord Jesus,
friend of God,
we thank you that you come and show us the ways of God,
the God who stretches out hands
in greeting and challenge,
liberating and blessing,
healing and raising to new life.

3 A deserted place

Read Mark 1:35–45.

> *In the morning, while it was still very dark he got up and went out to a deserted place, and there he prayed.* (Mark 1:35)

Mark introduces us to the picture of Jesus withdrawing to a remote place to pray, in the midst of his mission to the towns and villages of Galilee. For Jesus, the remote place, the hill country, the mountains, are essential places to give full undivided attention to the reality and will of God. The mountainside was closely associated in Jewish thinking with nearness of the revealing God. 'Moses went up to God and the Lord called to him from the mountain' (Exodus 19:3). Elijah is told: 'Go out and stand on the mountain before the Lord, for the Lord is about to pass by' (1 Kings 19:11). God is there revealed to Elijah not in wind, earthquake or fire, but in 'a sound of sheer silence' (1 Kings 19:12).

It is perhaps ironic that on the two occasions that Mark writes of Jesus withdrawing to a remote place people come and interrupt the time apart. Here in this passage Simon and his companions hunt for him and eventually find him (at which point he tells them that they must move on). The other mention of a remote place comes after the mission of the twelve. Alongside these two references to 'remote' places there are other times Jesus withdraws to pray: going up the mountain after the feeding of the five thousand (6:46), the mountain 'apart' in the story of the transfiguration (9:2) and the garden of Gethsemane (14:32).

The fact that only a few occasions are mentioned in Mark's gospel does not diminish the importance of this picture of Jesus alone and apart, finding an undisturbed space for his God. Developing from Mark's work, Luke stresses the importance of Jesus' times of prayer by including these moments of withdrawal at each key stage of his ministry, while Matthew records Jesus' teaching about prayer: 'whenever you pray, go into your room and shut the door and pray to your Father who is in secret and your Father who is in secret will reward you' (Matthew 6:6).

Finding our own place of withdrawal, whether it be a room in our home, a garden seat, a quiet corner in a church, a hillside or a retreat centre, is a necessary part of our prayer journey, whatever our situation or personality.

Reflect, picturing Jesus ahead of you, journeying into the desert

The dawn is yet to come, the darkness remains
   and while others sleep,
Jesus slips away to a deserted place.
And I follow at a distance to see what he is about.
There alone in that desert land, he watches and listens:
   the sun is rising yet the air remains cool and crisp;
   the sound of a single bird high in the sky
     echoes across the valley;
   the scent of dew on the stones and shrubs fills the air;
   and now sheer silence, deep and unbroken.
And there I see him pray:
   Jesus stands as the beloved before the love-giver,
   as the child in his parent's arms,
   the chosen one before the One who has chosen,
   now his oneness with the Living God is so clear.
The moment is there, hanging in the stillness:
   and now the moment is broken;
   the journey must continue;
   this good news, this deep joy, this glorious reckless love
     must be shared
   now and every day.

4 Healing and forgiveness

Read Mark 2:1–12.

> *Then some people came, bringing to him a paralysed man, carried by four of them. (Mark 2:3)*

The previous story ended with people 'coming to Jesus from every quarter'. The scene now focuses on a series of stories of particular people and the controversies that their encounters with Jesus caused. This is the first in a collection of 'controversy stories', which may have been drawn together by Mark or have already been in circulation.

As twenty-first-century Westerners, whose homes are our castles, we might well focus on the damage done by the man's friends to the roof, but this for Jesus shows their utter faith and trust, their determination to bring the man to him, whatever the difficulty. Jesus' first reaction on seeing the friends' trust and the man's need is not to heal the man physically. Instead, it is to declare his sins forgiven, not because those sins are the cause of his paralysis – as would have been believed by the culture of Jesus' time – or because they are some psychological block causing the paralysis, which might be our twenty-first-century way of looking at this. Jesus declares God's forgiveness because that is the man's greatest need and because that is what Jesus has come to do. This is Mark's message within the story: Jesus has the authority to bring God's forgiveness, God's restoration of relationship, and wishes to offer that forgiveness even before it is asked for. This is a real and mighty task and certainly not to be dismissed as easy glib words. Jesus asks, 'Which is easier?' – to say to the paralysed man, 'Your sins are forgiven', or, 'Stand up.' He will use that same word 'easier' to compare a camel going through the eye of a needle and a rich man entering the kingdom of God. Bringing God's forgiveness is harder, Jesus is implying, than getting a man who is totally paralysed to stand up; it is humanly impossible. The amazing grace of God – the God who does impossible things – means the harder reality of forgiveness is possible for all, though it will be immensely costly for Jesus, taking him ultimately to the cross.

The act of the friends makes the spiritual and physical restoration possible and as such is a symbol of all determined loving action of people for others and trust in God. Joel Marcus comments that the friends' faith and physical carrying of the man 'may relate to the Christian practice of intercessory prayer and the imperative of "bearing one another's burdens" (Gal 6:2)'.[50] We give thanks for those who have carried our burdens and brought us to the feet of Jesus, and we seek, in prayer and action, to do the same for others.

Reflect and pray

Let us praise God
for friends who stand beside us,
   those who carry us through the darkest of times,
   those who believe in us and for us,
   those who pray for our well-being
   and bring us to the Lord.

Let us praise God
for the work of healing,
   all who minister to the paralysed,
   surgeons, nurses, doctors and physiotherapists,
   encouraging each tiny step towards recovery,
   psychiatrists, counsellors and listeners,
   helping those traumatised and afraid.

Let us praise God
for words of forgiveness
that bring hope and healing deep within the human spirit.

Let us praise God
for the authority of Jesus to forgive,
to take from us
   the guilt that paralyses the spirit,
   the fear that hides all hope,
   the isolation that brings despair.

Let us praise God
for the work of healing in body, mind and spirit,
the work of human kindness and skill,
the work of divine compassion and grace.

5 From money table to meal table

Read Mark 2:13–22.

> *Jesus said, 'I have come to call not the righteous but sinners.' (Mark 2:17)*

Food is a recurring theme in Mark's gospel, reflecting the importance of sharing food in the Jewish faith and the central place of the Lord's Supper and fellowship meals within the young Church's life. Controversies begin again and again over food – who you can eat with, whether you eat or fast, when you eat, what you eat and whether you do so with ritually clean hands or not. Here the question is a matter of who one should share food with. The Pharisees, whose name means 'one separated from sin', regard Jesus as being reckless and likely to be contaminated by eating with those who were both ritually unclean and morally and religiously suspect.

Jesus has no such fears of contamination; he is the doctor who will bravely enter any house and reach out to anyone who is spiritually in need. His call of Levi involves the same simple phrase he used to call the fishermen: 'Follow me.' It sums up what discipleship is about for Mark: keeping company with Christ and following his leadership and his way. Unlike the paralysed man of the previous story, Levi, the tax collector and son of Alphaeus, is not sick in physical terms. However, he too is challenged to do a new thing – to stand up, leave behind his business and family connections and follow Jesus. As the paralysed man goes home, so Levi also goes home, inviting Jesus to go with him and to meet and eat with his friends. New life has entered Levi's life – in the shape of Jesus the great physician, whose name in the words of Charles Wesley is 'life and health and peace'.[51]

Reflect and pray

God of new beginnings and overflowing grace,
we thank you for Levi
the courageous one
who steps out of the confines of business
    and family connections
to follow Jesus with all the challenges that will bring.

We thank you for Levi
the welcoming one
who invites his friends to meet the Jesus
    who has entered his life.

We thank you for Levi
the dependent one
who knows that he cannot heal himself,
cannot start again by himself,
cannot forgive himself or find his own way,
but knows that Jesus can do this,
like a good doctor to heal a sick patient,
like a bridegroom to love the bride,
like fresh new clothes to replace those that are threadbare,
like new wine to bring joy to heart and soul.

We thank you for Levi
the glad one
who rejoices in the call of Jesus
in the best way he or we can,
with a meal for friends,
a celebration and a party,
not some stuffy event for the select few
but open to all who see their need
for that food that Jesus can give.

6 Stretching hands and hearts

Read Mark 2:23—3:6.

> *He was grieved at their hardness of heart and said to the man, 'Stretch out your hand.'* (Mark 3:5)

As we have already seen, Mark's gospel is full of controversy and conflict, revolving around key theological debates and the identity of Jesus. Here Jesus enters into a debate about the place of the Sabbath and how those Sabbath rules relate to human need. Like all rabbis of his time he uses his intellect to enter this debate. He draws from precedent, giving the example of David and his companions who ate the bread of the presence (1 Samuel 21:1–6) and makes comparisons, noting the Sabbath exceptions made in cases when life itself is at risk. It is clear that not all are willing to enter into such healthy debate. The unlikely alliance of Herodians and Pharisees – the former unclean in strict terms to the latter – plot to close down the debate, by getting rid of Jesus, the first hint of the plot and passion to come.

However, the story makes clear that for Jesus this argument is not simply a theoretical or intellectual debate. Jesus draws on his emotions, as he looks round at those whose hearts and minds are made up and who will not listen to reason. His anger and grief at this hardness of heart propels him forward into action, alongside his compassion for the man in need. He refuses to allow the Sabbath rules to become an excuse to do nothing in the face of human suffering. Imagining his anger and grief in our praying can be a valuable antidote for the compassion fatigue that we in Western society frequently experience. Our anger often revolves around those things that injure our sense of importance and worth, our grief over our losses; Jesus' anger and grief is focused on the needs of the ordinary people around him.

Reflect and pray

Lord of all my days,
guard my heart from stubbornness and fear.

Let me hear your piercing challenge
to a faith that shrivels, becoming narrow and hard
like a flower that is closed,
like a bud that will not open.

Let me feel your anger
at those who close their minds
to broken humanity and to your ways.

Let me know your deep distress.

Let me receive your healing,
restoring shrivelled hands and heart to usefulness,
stretching my mind into wonder,
my life into that abundance
you desire for me.

7 Sent out

Read Mark 3:7–19.

> *He went up the mountain and called to him those whom he wanted and they came to him.* (Mark 3:13)

Mark now enlarges the scene, telling how crowds came to Jesus from far and wide – from Galilee (the area Jesus has been preaching in), Judaea and Jerusalem (the heart of the nation), but also from outlying areas too where the population is much more mixed. From the crush of the crowd, the demands of healing and the cries of the unclean spirits, Jesus withdraws up the mountain calling 'those whom he wanted'. The mountain is a sacred setting, the place in the Exodus story where Moses declares God's covenant with his people. Now Mark uses these associations to speak of a newly formed people of God, 'the twelve' echoing the twelve sons of Jacob and the twelve tribes of Israel.

The twelve are representative of the whole community – of which Mark's own church is part. Their three tasks here are to be companions of Jesus (learning and observing him), to be sent out to speak his message and to have authority to drive out demons. Mark no doubt saw those apostolic tasks as being required of his own church community amid the challenges they faced. In our own situation the Christian community is still called to stay close to their founder, to speak his message and to exercise his authority in the work of confronting evil, healing, caring and reconciling.

The twelve are not called because they are perfect people or supreme disciples. Each has a unique personality; each is named, their maleness simply reflecting the culture and assumptions of the time. Jesus' renaming of Simon as Peter (Rock) is full of irony, given the story Mark tells later of Peter's denial. James and John's nickname, 'Thunder Brothers' (Daryl Schmidt's translation[52]), was no doubt appropriate too. Mark sees the twelve as very fallible, yet all the same called by Jesus to be a new community, to be close to him, to speak in his name and to act in his power. The Church today, with its many wounds and divisions, foibles and fallibility, is called to do the same.

Reflect and pray

So, Lord, this is what you call the twelve to be:
those that are with you and those that are sent out
to preach and act with your power,
to unify your followers as one new nation.

Lord, forgive your Church today
for its failures and foolishness.
When we fail to be with you,
draw us back to your self.
When we fail to speak or act in your gracious power,
reinvigorate us with your Spirit.
When we forget your commission
    and become instead a cosy club,
send us out once more.
When we become so divided
    that we fail to show your oneness,
remake us in your image.
When we desert or betray your way,
confront us with your cross
and bring us new hope and life.

8 Our brother Jesus

Read Mark 3:20–35.

'Whoever does the will of God is my brother and sister and mother.'
(Mark 3:35)

The sense of conflict that has underlain the gospel continues as Jesus meets misunderstanding, suspicion and opposition. For Mark there is a spiritual battle going on which is real and costly, though he is convinced that the ultimate victor is assured – the strong man of evil is being bound and his victims are being freed. The conflict is between good and evil, God and Satan, and is played out in numerous ways in the motives, words and actions of human beings.

Jesus' own family members are not immune from being involved in this struggle – and choosing the right or wrong side of it – just as the disciples themselves sway between the two poles, following or running away, trusting or giving into fear. Family is a crucial part of the world Jesus inhabits and at times Jesus speaks of the importance of family responsibilities. The fifth commandment, 'Honour your father and your mother', is part of his world-view and in chapter 7 he attacks the undermining of this responsibility by the religious practice of some Pharisees in declaring resources as 'Corban' and so not available for family members in need.

However, despite this respect for family, the story of this passage shows the limits of the family relationship when seen in the perspective of God's coming kingdom. Jesus' family come to take charge of him, seeing him either as out of his mind or as being thought by others to be so; it is not clear whether 'they' refers to Jesus' relatives or other people. In the face of misunderstanding by his family and accusations from the scribes that he is in league with the devil, Jesus uses his strongest language. Mark has from the beginning stressed that Jesus lives and works through the power of God's Spirit – the Holy Spirit – and to confuse or malign this Spirit as some magical unclean and satanic spirit is the ultimate blasphemy and twisting of truth.

When Jesus' mother and brothers come to call him away, he points to the disciples and listeners around him, claiming them and 'whoever does the will of God' as part of his gloriously extended family. This 'doing the will of God' is the keystone of Jesus' life, as he will pray in Gethsemane when he faces the cross; those who do likewise are his brothers and sisters, here and now.

Reflect and pray

God, who is to us the great Abba,
Father and Mother to us all,
we thank you for our dear brother Jesus.
We praise you for your Spirit
at work so gracefully in him
and touching lives in our day too.
Guard us from all falsehood and distortion.
Keep us from the great sin of seeing good as evil
    and evil as good.
Free us from all that binds us firm,
that we may know your will for our lives
    in the complexity of life
and act on what we know.
Help us to dare to live as your children,
brothers and sisters, parents and children,
within that new reality that Jesus brings,
your kingdom of grace, your circle of love.

9 *Seed of grace*

Read Mark 4:1–20.

> *And these are the ones sown on the good soil; they hear the word and accept it and bear fruit, thirty and sixty and a hundredfold.*
> (*Mark 4:20*)

Mark has made clear that Jesus' teaching touches his hearers in a powerful way. He has given us a taste of Jesus' teachings in the encounters that have already taken place, particularly arising from controversies and conflicts with his opponents. He has begun to show that not all respond positively to what Jesus has to say. Now he gives us a sizeable collection of Jesus' teaching as it takes the form of parables. The word literally means 'throwing alongside',[53] and here it is the mystery of the kingdom of God that is thrown alongside the picture of a farmer scattering seed, some failing to grow properly and some bearing fruit.

The word is powerful and the picture of the seed sown speaks of that power in the thirtyfold, sixtyfold and hundredfold harvest produced. For the first century, and even for our own, this is an extraordinary harvest; as Daryl Schmidt points out, 'a tenfold harvest would have been a good harvest'.[54] The ultimate success of the harvest – the realising of God's kingdom – is assured, but the word-sowing is not without difficulty. Just as the farmer scatters the seed liberally, some falling by the wayside, so the word of God will in places encounter rejection and frustration. Why some soil for the word is good and other not so is fully answered neither by Jesus nor by Mark, but the reality of the different reactions is seen as the way things are.

Jesus' quoting of Isaiah's prophecy reflects this mystery to some extent, though it is clear that for Mark the disciples at this point are as much in the dark about the parable's meaning as the crowd. None can assume that they are either good or bad soil; disciples fall by the wayside while a Roman centurion acclaims Jesus as Son of God; the high priest fails to recognise the Christ, yet a scribe is found to be 'not far from the kingdom' and a council member provides a tomb for Jesus' body. Crowd and disciples alike are challenged to develop a greater receptiveness to God's word of grace – to listen with both ears, to look deeply, to allow that word to take real root, to grow healthily and to bear a good harvest.

Reflect and pray

Seed of grace, Word of life
deep within us,
be warmed by the Great Sun,
be watered by the Great Spirit,
be nurtured by the Great Shepherd.

Seed of grace, Word of life,
do not let your hope be taken from us;
do not let our joy in you evaporate;
do not let love for you be choked by self-concern.

Seed of grace, Word of life,
bear a great harvest in hearts open to your goodness,
in lives touched and healed and changed,
multiplying your bounty again and again,
until your kingdom comes.

10 The growing mustard seed

Read Mark 4:21–33.

> 'With what can we compare the kingdom of God, or what parable
> shall we use of it?' (Mark 4:30)

The parables of Jesus are not puzzles to confuse or to solve, but
means of opening up the great secret – the work of God among us,
the kingdom of God. They do not define that kingdom in precise
doctrinal terms, but rather provide pictures to point us in the right
direction and enable us to glimpse its wonder.

The parable of the mustard seed comes within a collection of
sayings and parables that were brought together either over the
years of telling and retelling by the early Christian community or
by Mark himself. They all connect with the themes of hiddenness
and growth, the grace of God and the need for response. The lamp
is not meant to be placed under a bowl or bed. The seed is not
meant to be kept for ever underground, but is to grow, producing
stalk, ear and full grain.

The growth is a source of wonder, both as a process – 'the man
knows not how' (4:27) – and in its results – 'becomes the greatest
of all shrubs' (4:32). The source of the growth is beyond human
control: it is pure gift – the grace of God. The kingdom of God
will grow whether we sleep or get up; its coming 'depends on the
invisible but unstoppable processes of God'.[55] Yet a human
response is called for within these sayings and stories – a willingness to listen and receive, a readiness to respond when the time is
right and a desire to accept and use the gift that is given. This is
what the kingdom of God is like – a tiny seed yet with immense
power within it to grow, to give light, to nourish and provide
ultimate shelter.

Reflect and pray

Mustard seed God,
you work in hidden ways,
sowing your seed of life
in hearts and minds,
cultures and communities.

We praise you for your hidden ways.
Here are no pyrotechnics, no great trumpet calls,
no visions of blazing light or glorious victories.
Instead you point us to a tiny seed,
hidden and vulnerable,
sown in the muddy soil of life,
growing among us and changing our ways for good,
growing beyond measure and control,
a wondrous tree that gives shade to all
parched by the world's ways.
We praise you, we thank you for the kingdom seed,
Jesus, who gives life again and again.

11 The storm and the questions

Read Mark 4:35—5:20.

> *Jesus woke up and rebuked the wind, and said to the sea, 'Peace, be still.' (Mark 4:39)*

Questions have echoed down the pages of Mark's story, guiding us towards the secret of Jesus' identity, dealing with great debates within the community of faith and helping to learn what Jesus asks of us, the hearer or reader of the gospel. There are an extraordinary number of questions asked (119 in the gospel at my counting) and this may reflect the form of teaching within Judaism and the early Church, such as the Passover questions and the baptismal catechism. Questions are asked of Jesus by the demons and unclean spirits ('have you come to destroy us?', 1:24), by Jesus' opponents ('by what authority?', 11:28), by would-be disciples ('what must I do to inherit eternal life?', 10:17) and the disciples themselves ('then who can be saved?' 10:26). Even more significant are the questions Jesus asks, for these challenge a response not only from the characters within the story, but from us the audience. Praying with the gospel will involve listening out for these questions and reflecting on what they may be asking of us in our own situation.

The stories of the stilling of the storm and the stilling of the demon-possessed man raise plenty of questions for us Western Christians, with all our modern-day attitudes and advantages. They also contain significant questions. That of the disciples, 'Teacher, do you not care that we are perishing?', has a strong flavour of the Psalms. There the psalmist sometimes accuses God of sleeping while Israel suffers: 'Rouse yourself! Why do you sleep, O Lord?' (Psalm 44:23). The disciples' cry speaks vividly to all situations where people feel helpless, bewildered and deserted by God. It is a way of venting anger at God, or Jesus his representative, which is a very valid part of praying. Jesus' own questions to the disciples in turn challenge this anger and lack of trust: 'Why are you afraid? Have you still no faith?' (4:40). Legion's demons ask their own question of Jesus and give him the exalted title 'Son of the Most High God', while Jesus responds with the very simple question, 'What is your name?' In what follows, the dehumanised name of Legion is destroyed and the man's true identity is restored. He is human again, clothed, in his right mind and sent back home to his friends to tell them what his merciful God has done.

Reflect and pray

Our minds, Lord, are full of questions:
   How was the storm stilled?
   What were the spirits that bound Legion?
   Why did the pigs die in such numbers?
   Why did you send the man home?
And questions echo through these stories,
the desperate question of the disciples:
   Teacher, do you not care that we are perishing?
And yours to them,
   when the wind had been rebuked
and the sea had been told to be still,
   your questions to us too:
   Why are you afraid?
   Have you still no faith?

Legion's demons recognise and ask:
   What have you to do with me, Jesus, Son of God?
As if claiming that this man is beyond your reach,
outside your territory of care,
but you ask the human question,
the question that recognises the man
   behind the broken chains,
the bruises, the howls and nakedness,
   the madness and isolation.
You ask:
   What is your name?
And from there you draw this broken man back
   to his humanity,
to a conversation,
   sitting together in peace.

From there you draw this rejected scrap of humanity
     back into his community,
encouraging him simply to go back to his friends
     (he has friends, thank God)
and to tell them how much the Lord has done for him
and what mercy he has shown.

Lord Jesus, speak your peace to us.
Still our questions.
Name us and renew our humanity,
that we may proclaim all you have done for us
and that great mercy you have shown us.

12 Hem and hand

Read Mark 5:21–43.

> *He took her by the hand and said, 'Talitha cum,' which means, 'Little girl, get up!'* (Mark 5:41)

Mark in typical fashion interweaves two stories, placing the healing of the woman with the haemorrhage in the centre of the story of Jairus' dying daughter. It is a form we see in novels and films today, there to heighten suspense and to encourage us to make connections. Mark further connects the two stories by telling us that the child was twelve years old, the same number of years that the woman had been bleeding.

Each story shows Jesus responding to a plea for help. Jairus, an important person in the town as one of the leaders of the synagogue, voices that plea in a form that is almost a prayer. Falling at Jesus' feet he begs repeatedly: 'My little daughter is at the point of death. Come and lay your hands on her, so that she may be made well, and live' (5:23). The woman, on the other hand, is unnamed and unseen. She is in effect dying too; she has spent all she has on doctors and only grown worse. In her culture, of course, her flow of blood has made her unclean and untouchable, separated and voiceless. Her plea has no words; it is the secret silent touching of the hem of Jesus' cloak, an immensely powerful picture of prayer.

In each of the intertwined stories Jesus says a ridiculous thing that points to the strange work of God. In the face of the pressing crowd, he asks, 'Who touched me?' and enables the woman to 'come clean'. In the face of a child at death's door and a crowd of professional weepers, he says, 'She's not dead but sleeping' and takes her by the hand; his gentle whisper 'Talitha cum', recorded in Aramaic, no doubt having a powerful effect on the listeners to the gospel. Here is Mark's humour and irony at work to make us question our assumptions and see Jesus in a new and surprising way as he touches our lives.

Reflect and pray

God of all,
we hold before you
the desperate of our world:
    parents anxious for a sick child,
    torn apart by seeing their son or daughter
    wracked by pain,
    fearing for the worst,
    people who live day by day with incurable illness.

We hold before you
those who voice their longings in words and prayers,
who look to you for help.

We hold before you
those who can find no words,
yet reach out to you all the same.

Come to their aid, dear Lord.
Give them the faith they need for the hardest days,
that fear may be kept at bay.
Keep their love strong,
    a love for a child that can echo your love,
    a love for life that can echo your love too.
May they know your peace in life,
    in death and in life restored.
We ask in the name of Jesus, who bled on a cross
    and whom you raised up to life,
turning lament into laughter,
grey bleakness into glorious wonder.

Thanks be to you, Eternal God,
for your gift beyond words.

13 Rejection and mission

Read Mark 6:1–13.

> *He called the twelve and began to send them out two by two, and gave them authority over unclean spirits.* (*Mark 6:7*)

Jesus returns home to Nazareth and initially seems to produce a response of wonder and awe very similar to that at the beginning of his ministry (1:21–28). Then Jesus' fame had spread, but now in his own town amazement leads to resentment and rejection, as his townsfolk dismiss him as being the carpenter. He's just Mary's son and his brothers and sisters are their neighbours. Jesus remembers a local saying: 'Prophets are not without honour except in their hometown.' Their ready-made assumptions and closed thinking block his work among them; 'he could do no deed of power there', though Mark then adds, 'except that he laid his hands on a few sick people and cured them' (6:5). Jesus' focus is still on those who know their need of God. As he told the Pharisees when they grumbled over his eating with tax collectors and sinners: 'Those who are well have no need of a physician, but those who are sick; I have come to call not the righteous but sinners' (2:17).

Far from causing Jesus to draw back, the experience of frustration in his own town, and shock at their unbelief (6:5), brings about a new stage in his mission to the area.

He calls the twelve, just as he called them earlier to leave their nets (1:16–20) and commissioned them on the mountainside (3:13–19). For Mark, Jesus' call is not a one-off event, but a repeated claim on the lives of his followers. It both develops, as new tasks unfold, and needs to be renewed, as failures and faithlessness slow his followers down.

The twelve are commissioned to share in Jesus' work of proclaiming the kingdom of God in word and action. The key message remains that of repentance – turning round – and the key action that of healing – freeing people from all that oppresses them. The tools for the task are simplicity and integrity. They are to take a staff to defend themselves and remind them of the shepherd ('I fear no evil for you are with me; your rod and staff – they comfort me', Psalm 23:4) and some oil to bathe and heal the injured ('You anoint my head with oil', Psalm 23:5). The twelve have great success, but Jesus' words are there to remind them that rejection is part of the story, too, just as he had experienced in his own home town.

Reflect and pray

In the journey of life,
Lord Jesus,
be a staff to me.
  A staff to lean upon when I am lame,
  struggling to keep walking with you.
  A staff to defend me
  against the dangers around me and within,
  the dark voices that call me to turn back.
  A staff to point out the way ahead,
  to direct and encourage.
  A staff to remind me of Moses and David
  and all who have found hope replacing fear
  and God's comfort on the darkest paths.
In the journey of life,
Lord Jesus,
be a staff to me
and all whom you send out in your name,
to speak in your name,
to stand out against evil,
to share in your healing work,
to pour out your goodness and mercy.

14 Death interrupts

Read Mark 6:14–29.

> *Immediately the king sent a soldier of the guard with orders to bring John's head. He went and beheaded him in the prison, brought his head on a platter and gave it to the girl.* (*Mark 6:28*)

John the Baptist played a crucial role in the launching of the gospel and now the story of his death points forward to its end, the summary execution he suffers foreshadowing the fate Jesus will endure. It is the most brutal of interruptions to the story Mark is telling, coming without warning immediately after the story of the successful mission of the disciples. Death is portrayed here at its most mocking and brutal – a decapitated, lifeless head on a platter brought into a party as if some new delicacy for the banquet. Joel Marcus describes it as a scene of Gothic horror with 'overtones of cannibalism'.[56]

Herod's birthday becomes John's death-day. There is no hint here of a hope beyond death (that must wait for Jesus); John's disciples simply 'came and took his body and laid it in the tomb'. Death is shown at its most real and violent, but also evil in its most twisted form. There is Herod's weakness and pride, Herodias' bitterness and deadly hatred, the manipulation of and by the daughter – a girl being used and using – and the guards simply 'following orders'. We have seen it all before and since. This is our world, and against these powers of death and darkness, violence and injustice Jesus comes to enlist us in his mission of life-giving.

Herod's 'Ask whatever you wish and I will give it' is a mockery of prayer and should warn us against making prayer into a pursuit of our own agendas (God as the heavenly Father Christmas or Fairy Godmother). Herod's troubled mind results in him seeing Jesus as John raised from the dead, a reminder that the Herods of this world will not have the final word. In Desmond Tutu's famous words: 'Good is stronger than evil; love is stronger than hate; light is stronger than darkness; life is stronger than death. Victory is ours, through him who loves us.'[57]

Reflect and pray

A girl dancing.
A drunken promise.
And a man is dead,
his head lying stupidly
on a platter, the final insult.
The bloody suddenness of it
would shock us to the bone,
if we were not so hardened.
Sudden violent deaths are so much
part of our world and our history:
the purges, the gas chambers,
　　the trenches, the killing fields,
the soldier standing on the IED,
　　the teenager and the lunging knife,
the plunging aeroplane, the running child
　　and speeding car.
Death interrupts suddenly and fiercely,
leaving tattered pieces in its wake
　　and numbed grieving hearts.

John's disciples came and took the body,
burying the remains to return some dignity
to the man who had inspired them.
And Herod remained troubled and confused, seeing ghosts,
seeing John in Jesus' work.

Lord, in a world where death can come so viciously,
　　without rhyme or reason,
give us courage
to hold to faith,
to speak out against evil,
to seek justice,
to make peace,
and to keep hope alive.

15 Green grass

Read Mark 6:30–44.

> *As he went ashore he saw a great crowd; and he had compassion on them, because they were like sheep without a shepherd. (Mark 6:34)*

There is no doubt of the importance of the story of the feeding of the five thousand to the young Church; it is one of the few miracles recorded in all four gospels. Mark tells the story with great care to draw out its meaning and value. He links it to the story of the mission of the twelve. His opening description of Jesus taking the apostles away to 'a deserted place' to rest echoes Jesus' own withdrawal to pray in 1:35.

The story of the great feeding is one that is rooted in time and place and yet also speaks to the gospel-hearers of past, present and future. It points back to the Exodus experience of the people of Israel in the wilderness and God's feeding of them with the manna (Exodus 16), and to Elisha's feeding of the one hundred (2 Kings 4:42–44). It points forward to the eschatological end times and the fulfilment of God's kingdom, pictured by the prophet Isaiah as a great feast (Isaiah 25:6). And it points to the present in the blessing of food and the pattern of the Eucharist – the blessing, breaking and sharing of the loaves.

Amid all this Mark notes that the crowds sit down on the green grass, a tiny detail that Matthew and Luke omit as unimportant when drawing on Mark's materials to write their own gospels. It could be simply a preserved memory that had been handed down by the first eyewitnesses, or again it may be included by Mark because it points his readers towards springtime, renewal and the words of Psalm 23: 'he makes me lie down in green pastures.' After all, that is where the story begins – Jesus seeing the crowd and having compassion for them, 'because they were like sheep without a shepherd'. He has come, in God's name, to be the compassionate Shepherd to lead his people.

Reflect and pray

For times of rest and places that refresh
and the One to whom we can open our hearts:
    We thank you, life-giving God.
For the green grass, growing so abundantly
when the rains come and the parched land drinks its fill:
    We thank you, life-giving God.
For the crowds of people, women and men, young and old,
awkward and beautiful, battered and anxious,
    each with their gifts and needs:
    We thank you, life-giving God.
For the One who looks at all with compassion,
whose words bring life and whose hands break bread:
    We thank you, life-giving God.
For the gift of bread, offered and blessed,
    torn apart and shared among many
to nourish and sustain, bringing strength and joy:
    We thank you, life-giving God.
For nothing wasted, crumbs gathered in a basket
and none left hungry:
    We thank you, life-giving God.
For signs of your overflowing kingdom,
    glimpses of your abundant will,
the taste of your all-embracing banquet:
    We thank you, life-giving God.
So by your Spirit help us to rest and to be fed,
to look at all with compassion
    and leave none lost or hungry,
for the sake of our great shepherd, Jesus Christ. Amen.

16 Passing glory

Read Mark 6:45–56.

'Take heart, it is I; do not be afraid.' (Mark 6:50)

The feeding of the five thousand had many echoes of the Exodus story of Moses and the people of Israel in the wilderness, and echoes continue to reverberate in this story that concludes the section, linked by Jesus' dismissal of the disciples and the crowd and his going up the mountain to pray. The story places Jesus as the initiator of every positive action: he sees the disciples struggling with the storm, he comes towards them, he speaks to them, he gets into the boat. The disciples, on the other hand, struggle throughout the story, first with their rowing in the storm, then afraid they are seeing a ghost, then terrified, then astounded because their hearts were hardened.

In the middle of the story is the strange phrase that Jesus 'intended to pass them by'. Scholars have long debated the meaning of the phrase, but a widely held view is that it echoes the story found in Exodus 33:17–34 where God reveals his glory to Moses: 'The Lord passed before him' (Exodus 33:34). The same theme is taken up in the story of Elijah in the wilderness (1 Kings 19:11–13) where Elijah is told: 'Go stand on the mountain before the Lord, for the Lord is about to pass by' (1 Kings 19:11) and after wind, earthquake and fire God reveals his true presence in a 'still small voice' (1 Kings 19:12 AV) or 'a sound of sheer silence' (1 Kings 19:12 NRSV). As Joel Marcus comments, 'the verb *parelthein* ("to pass", "to pass by") became almost a technical term for a divine epiphany in the Septuagint'.[58]

Mark wants to make clear that this encounter of Jesus and his disciples is an epiphany moment and Jesus' words underline this divine opening: 'Take heart, it is I', or literally, 'I am', itself an echo of the divine name revealed to Moses in the Exodus story (and a

theme that John's gospel develops in the series of 'I am' sayings of
Jesus). 'God said to Moses, "I am who I am" ' (Exodus 3:14). Here
in Jesus the disciples are confronted with the divine 'I am'.

Reflect and pray

We praise you,
God of mountain and mystery,
sea and storm,
presence and peace.

You were there with Moses,
opening up a glimpse of your glory and goodness,
through the cleft of a rock,
merciful and gracious,
abounding in love,
steadfast in faithfulness.

You were there with Elijah,
speaking out in the sound of sheer silence,
a silence that came through the storm and earthquake
and quenched the fire.

You were there in Jesus,
on mountain top and stormy lake,
there in his words:
'Take heart, it is I; do not be afraid',
words that calmed the raging wind
and touched hardened hearts.

You are here through the Spirit,
opening up glimpses of glory and goodness,
speaking in the sound of sheer silence,
making yourself known as the One
who can touch hardened hearts.

We praise you,
God of mountain and mystery,
sea and storm,
presence and peace.

17 Lip service

Read Mark 7:1–23.

> 'This people honours me with their lips but their hearts are far from me.' (Mark 7:6)

The Gospel and the ministry of Jesus is rooted in the story, traditions and faith of Judaism and many of the debates that the gospel addresses were current within first-century Judaism as a whole. One such debate was the purity regulations. Washing hands before every meal was a matter not simply of hygiene (think of the procedure now necessary before entering a hospital!), it was a matter of religious purity. The nations' priests had long followed the regulations, but the Pharisees in their zeal wanted them extended to all the people.

Jesus' response is to go deeper. First he questions whether his opponents are really showing a greater love for God by their demands. Then he tells his disciples that the inner life – the clean heart – and the actions that flow from that are far more important than the exterior show – the clean hands. He challenges the use of religion to avoid human obligations, in what might be called the Corban scandal. He grieves over a faith that is about regulations and procedures, rather than a Spirit-driven living out of God's commandments.

Mark's conclusion, 'thus he declared all food clean', was a radical message in the mixed communities of the early Church, but more crucially it leads onto the message that all people are potentially clean too. People are defiled not by race or religion or genetics, but by hearts that become distorted and twisted and actions that both lead out from this and cause this distortion. The gospel's antidote to this human distortion is to turn round, seek God's mercy, follow Jesus and receive the Holy Spirit to cleanse and revive.

Reflect and pray

When we pay you lip service
while our hearts are far from you
and our agendas are fixed on ourselves:
    Lord, have mercy.
When we use every trick in the book
to evade our responsibilities
towards those who need us:
    Lord, have mercy.
When we make religion our own
and mould a mirror god
that looks all too familiar:
    Lord, have mercy.
When we focus on the external,
customs or the latest fashion, rituals or appearances,
and forget the need to tend our hearts:
    Lord, have mercy.
When our relationships go wrong,
tainted by greed and delusion,
defiled by pride and folly:
    Lord, have mercy.

Restore us not with whitewash
but from deep within,
for your mercy's sake. Amen.

18 Crumbs

Read Mark 7:24–30.

> *But she answered him, 'Sir, even the dogs under the table eat the children's crumbs.' (Mark 7:28)*

Jesus acts out his own time and culture and there is no escaping that fact. His priority instinctively is to his own Jewish people, yet there are signs within his own ministry of a wider concern for all peoples, inspired no doubt by the vision of Isaiah calling Israel to be 'a light to the nations' (Isaiah 49:6).

This fascinating story of Jesus' encounter with the Greek woman from Syrian Phoenicia is a significant moment in this enlarging of mission. Jesus is in Tyre, border country, where encounters with Gentiles are inevitable. At the same time, he wants the visit to be secret and when this is not possible his first reaction to the Gentile woman is dismissive.

He echoes the language of his time and people by referring to the Jews as children and the Gentiles as dogs. Commentators may say that it is said with a smile – gently rather than abusively – but we cannot wholly escape the harshness of the words, very typical of the attitude of his people at that time. It is the woman's wit and persistence (two necessary qualities of faith and prayer) that win Jesus over, enabling him to move forward towards that total mission – to be a light to all nations.

So we thank God for the unnamed Syro-Phoenician woman and men and women like her who have challenged constricted assumptions and narrow attitudes even among the greatest of human beings. It is perhaps ironic that in the sixteenth century Thomas Cranmer took those words 'crumbs from under the table'[59] as part of the inspiration for the great prayer of humble access. By that time Christianity was in the ascendancy and Jews regarded with hatred and contempt – dogs that should have no access. Jews were expelled from England in 1290 and not invited to return until 1655. Centuries of continued anti-Semitism across Europe led inextricably on to the horrors of the Nazi concentration camps – the attempted extermination of a whole race.

Reflect and pray

We come, God who has no favourites,
to give thanks for your all-embracing love
for Jew and Gentile, men and women,
    black and white, straight and gay,
      young and old.

We come, God who has no favourites,
to give thanks for your open table,
where none will be treated as dogs,
where all can eat as your beloved children.

We come, God who has no favourites,
to give thanks for this story of Jesus
    and the unnamed woman,
a moment of truth and grace
for them both and for us all.

We come, God who has no favourites,
to ask your help to confront our own prejudices
    and presumptions,
and to gain the grace to change our minds and our hearts.

We come, God who has no favourites,
to seek that light which is for all nations,
and to pray that your salvation may reach
    to the ends of the earth.

19 Be opened

Read Mark 7:31–37.

> *Then looking up to heaven, he sighed and said to him, 'Ephphatha',*
> *that is 'Be opened.' (Mark 7:34)*

Following on from the conversation with the Gentile woman,
Jesus now tours the Gentile region of Sidon and Decapolis and
there meets a man who needs his help to hear and speak. These are
two of the great requirements of Jesus' followers, that is, to hear
the word and to proclaim the good news. As in several of the
healing stories friends bring the man to Jesus, begging him to place
a healing hand on the man. The man cannot ask himself, cannot
hear what is being asked on his behalf – his helplessness is total.
Jesus takes him to one side, and like healers of his time uses the
crude elements of fingers, spittle and touch to begin his work.
Then comes the cry of 'Ephphatha', 'Be opened', a prayer and a
command that has an immediate effect. Just as he did in the tale of
Jairus' daughter (with Jesus' words 'talitha cum'), Mark retains the
memory of the Aramaic word; it has become lodged in the story as
a powerful, mysterious word and perhaps was still being used by
Mark's own Greek-speaking community in their ministry of
healing and exorcism. The man's ears are opened and tongue
released.

Absurdly Jesus then tells the man to tell no one, a characteristic
theme in Mark's story, but one that he knows will be broken here;
the man who has been given his tongue is not going to waste time
being silent. The word is out – now in the Gentile territory as it
was in Judaea. If joy is not a strong theme in Mark's gospel, then
wonder is, and following the healing of the deaf and mute man
that wonder turns into delight as the crowd acclaim Jesus with the
words, 'He has done everything well.' It is as if a new creation is
occurring, an echo of God's delight with the world he made: 'God

saw everything that he had made, and indeed, it was very good'
(Genesis 1:31). The opening of ears and the unshackling of
tongues is a sign of God's new beginning – God's kingdom
breaking into this world. Mark has the vision of Isaiah in mind:

> Then the eyes of the blind shall be opened.
>   and the ears of the deaf unstopped;
> then the lame shall leap like deer,
>   and the tongue of the speechless sing for joy. (Isaiah 35:6)

Reflect and pray

Lord Jesus, you have done everything well,
amazing us again and again
with the power and wisdom of your words,
the strength and compassion of your actions,
the depth and intensity of your being.

You have opened our ears
to the truth of God,
not the god of the theorist
or the totem of the religious,
but the Living God who is the source of true life.
You have opened our eyes
to see the world,
the world in the light of love,
not as a means to an end
or an object to be used,
but as a treasure of great wonder,
a place of great need.
You have opened our tongues
to sing in praise and to speak humbly of your grace.

Lord Jesus, you have done everything well:
accept our thanks and praise, our wonder and joy,
this and every day.

20 Sign and no sign

Read Mark 8:1–21.

> *He took the seven loaves, and after giving thanks he broke them and gave them to his disciples to distribute.* (Mark 8:6)

Mark is careful in his use of the stories he has gathered, ordering them in a continuous narrative that leads us rapidly from Galilee towards Jerusalem. So his use of a second story of a feeding miracle is something of a puzzle. Some scholars see the feeding of the five thousand as referring to a crowd of Jewish people (and the twelve loaves as relating to the twelve tribes of Israel), and then the feeding of the four thousand as relating to a crowd of Gentile people. The seven baskets might then be symbolic of wholeness – all nations (the seven days making a complete week). The reference to Jesus being in the region of Decapolis (7:31) might signify that Jesus was now in a Gentile region.

It is an attractive theory that recognises some of the symbolic nature of what is going on in the feeding miracles, but is not without difficulty. It may be that the repetition is simply there to emphasise the importance of this story with all its Exodus references.

It is all the more ironic that the story is followed by the demand of the Pharisees for a sign from heaven, again a link with the demands of Israel in the Exodus story. Jesus tells them that no sign will be given to this generation, yet in effect a sign has already been given and not only once. It has been repeated to give no room for doubt. The five thousand have been fed and the four thousand have been fed and baskets gathered of the remaining crumbs. The eucharistic overtones of both the feeding stories are strong: Jesus gives thanks, breaks the bread and gives it to his disciples to distribute. This is the great sign of the kingdom to be repeated again and again among his followers – and in Mark's own commu-

nity. And repeated not simply in the liturgical act of the Eucharist –
the Lord's Supper – but also in the daily acts of service which the
followers of Jesus undertake, in giving hospitality, providing food
for the hungry and support for widows and orphans. The twelve
baskets may after all represent the twelve apostles and the seven
baskets those seven chosen by the apostles to organise the daily
distribution of food (Acts 6:3).

So Mark's first hearers might recognise in the two great feeding
stories not only the compassionate ministry of Jesus (and resulting
miracles of multiplication), but also echoes both of the feeding
with manna in Exodus and the present-day life of their own
church community, celebrating the Eucharist and distributing
food to the hungry.

Reflect and pray

Like the Pharisees we demand signs, dear Lord:
signs that you are real and at work among us,
signs that you care and hear our prayers.
Yet you sigh and tell us:
No sign will be given.
No knock-out proof that you are with us and at work.
Instead you take bread and give thanks,
blessing your God and ours.
You give and call your friends to help in the giving.
And as we are fed,
and as we find that many others are fed too,
    thousands upon thousands,
our hearts are softened,
our eyes are cleared
and our ears are opened.
We remember how in every generation you have done this,
feeding so many that we could never count,
calling so many to share in the task of feeding your world.
Keep us from failing to see or understand.
Keep us from hardening our hearts or closing our ears.
Speak your word of thanks, your word of compassion.

21 *Partial vision*

Read Mark 8:22—9:1.

'For those who want to save their life will lose it, and those who lose their life for my sake, and the sake of the Gospel, will save it.'
(Mark 8:35)

A new stage in the gospel story opens up with Jesus' first prediction of what lies ahead of him in Jerusalem and it follows on from Peter's confession that Jesus is the Christ, the Messiah. Having received Peter's words – accepting them but wanting the disciples not to tell anyone – Jesus explains that he will not be the kind of Messiah they are expecting. Instead of grabbing political power and releasing Israel from Roman rule, he instead will face rejection and death – and then new life. Mark is not simply focused on the passion; the resurrection is spoken of in each of the three passion predictions.

Peter (and readers since) focuses on the prediction of suffering and death, and for Peter this is unacceptable; such a fate would be a sign of God's curse on Jesus, not blessing. In typically forthright fashion he rebukes Jesus, only to be in turn rebuked by Jesus.

Jesus goes on to tell Peter and the disciples that this act of self-giving on the cross, which is uniquely his as the suffering Christ, is yet at the same time a pattern for all who come after him: they must take up their cross and follow him. Peter has seen, recognising Jesus as Messiah, but not seen, refusing to accept Jesus' way of the cross. In this he is like the blind man whose story is told immediately before Peter's confession. His sight is restored in stages; he sees, but at first people look like trees. Mark has once again used a miracle of renewed vision to introduce a lesson about discipleship – the need for God to open our eyes.

Reflect and pray

God of perfect vision,
we see yet we do not see;
   a mist covers our hearts,
   a self-concern distorts our vision,
   a lack of imagination narrows our view of the world.
We beg for your touch
to liberate us from our blindness
that we may see Jesus,
   the promised Messiah,
   the man of the cross,
   the one who loses his life to save ours.
We beg for your touch again to clear our vision,
that we may see people not as objects – trees in the way –
but truly as your children, unique, vulnerable, dear to you.
We beg for your touch again,
that we may not only see, but that we may follow,
   forgetting ourselves,
   losing ourselves,
   giving ourselves,
   in the tasks you have for us this day.

22 Glimpse of glory

Read Mark 9:2–13.

Six days later Jesus took with him Peter and John and James and led them up a high mountain apart, by themselves. (Mark 9:2)

The story of the transfiguration marks a crucial staging post in the gospel, following on from Peter's declaration of Jesus as the Messiah and Jesus' first announcement of the passion that lies ahead for him. Unusually, Mark provides a definite time link, 'six days later', to make sure his readers know the stories are connected. This may also echo the story of Moses' ascent of Mount Sinai after six days (Exodus 24:16). Jesus takes his inner circle – Peter, John and James – who were present at the raising of Jairus' daughter (5:37) and will be there beside him when he prays in the garden (14:33).

On the mountain they enter into a vision of Jesus' glory, first in his transformation by divine light, then in his conversation with the prophets Moses and Elijah and finally in the divine mystery and voice itself. The voice that had spoken to Jesus at his baptism now speaks to the three terrified disciples, their terror once again an indication by Mark that extraordinary divine things are happening within and around Jesus. The words are almost the same, again reflecting the language of Isaiah: 'This is my Son, the Beloved', but now the key commandment is added: 'listen to him'. For Mark this is the key to Christian discipleship, the key to his gospel and the key to prayer: listen to Jesus.

This is the lesson that Peter takes the rest of the gospel learning. Here on the mountain he had suggested building tabernacles to somehow preserve the glorious experience. Jesus, however, will not be preserved or trapped in this way; he is the one who calls people to follow, the one who moves on and the one who journeys to Jerusalem, to the cross and beyond. John and James will also have to learn to listen to Jesus, as he points them away from self-glorification to self-giving. The glimpse of glory on the mountain directs them and us towards Jesus and the way ahead.

Reflect and pray

Lead us to the mountain, Great God,
the majestic mountain that shows us our smallness
raising our spirits and enlarging our minds.

Lead us to the light, Great God,
the dazzling light that reveals the goodness of Jesus
piercing the darkness of our doubts and fears.

Lead us to the vision, Great God,
the glorious vision of the lawgiver, the prophet and the Son
bound together in love for you and the world.

Lead us to the mystery, Great God,
the cloud of unknowing, the shadow of your being
stretching over us, like a tender hand.

Lead us to that point, Great God,
where we can truly listen,
truly hear the word of Christ
for our world at this moment.

Lead us down the mountain, Great God,
to the place of service,
the place where faith must work,
hope must be held, love must be shared.

23 *I believe, help my unbelief*

Read Mark 9:14–29.

> *Immediately the father of the child cried out, 'I believe, help my unbelief!'* (*Mark 9:24*)

Mark continues to be influenced by the story of Moses as he tells the story of Jesus' ministry. Just as Moses returns to the camp to find the people of Israel have lost trust in God (Exodus 32) so Jesus, on coming down from the mountain, discovers the other disciples have failed to be able to help a father and his child, and an argument is raging between them and the scribes. The atmosphere of divine presence and light has moved to one of dark grumblings and shifting blame. Jesus' response is one of deep lament: 'you faithless generation, how long must I be among you?' (9:19).

Yet lament moves on to action as Jesus puts to one side his own inner disappointment and anguish and directs his attention to the boy and his father. The conversation leads step by step to a challenge to trust, to which the father cries: 'I believe, help my unbelief.' It is one of the great affirmations of the gospels, a cry deep from the heart. Roland Riem focuses on this story as he explores power and vulnerability and sees the father's words as 'both a confession of trust in a hidden God and a confession of human helplessness before God provoked by Christ's words'.[60] It is both an expression of faith and a prayer for faith. The healing of the son that follows echoes the healing of Jairus' daughter and again ends with Jesus taking the child by the hand and raising him to his feet; again a pointer to resurrection. Power and vulnerability have met and done so in the conjoining of prayer – the father's prayer of faith seeking faith and Jesus' prayer of compassion and grace. The disciples are told not to presume that they have special powers, but

to pray; when they ask why they were unable to help the boy they
are told by Jesus: 'This kind can only come out through prayer'
(9:29).

Reflect and pray

God of powerful vulnerability,
we thank you for the praying of Jesus,
filling his encounter with a heart-torn parent
    and a broken boy
with resurrection power.

We hold before you all whom the Church has failed,
    by weakness of prayer or the abuse of power,
    by the failure to listen or the unwillingness
        to become involved,
    by lack of imagination or narrowness of minds.
Too many cries have gone unheard.
Too many children have lives bound or broken.

God of powerful vulnerability,
renew your people in this time of bewildering change.
Cast out our fear and faithlessness.
Bring us to our knees,
    that with a desperate father of another age,
    we too may cry,
'We believe, help our unbelief',
and like the boy, be raised to our feet,
to share in your work of powerful vulnerability.

24 The greatest

Read Mark 9:30–50.

> *But they were silent, for on the way they had argued with one*
> *another who was the greatest. (Mark 9:34)*

A second time Jesus tells his friends of what lies ahead for him at
Jerusalem – rejection, death and new life – and once again they do
not understand. Their journey continues, now bringing Jesus to
his home area again. When they are at home – a place linked with
teaching – Jesus asks them what they have been arguing about on
the way. They are silent, for they were arguing about who was the
greatest.

Spiritual comparisons and rivalry seem to have dogged the early
disciples and the young Church. Mark includes several references
to this, because no doubt they affected his church community, just
as they continue to damage the Church in our own times. Oscar
Wilde told a story of a devout hermit being tested and taunted by
demons without success. The chief demon tells the others that he
knows how it is to be done and quietly whispers in the monk's ear,
'Your brother has been made Bishop of Alexandria', at which
point the hermit's serene face darkens with malignant jealousy.[61]

Jesus suggests that the disciples learn how to welcome a child, a
non-person in their eyes whom they would ignore or send away,
and learn from this true human worth. He also suggests amputa-
tion, not literally of foot, hand or eye, but a similarly drastic cutting
out of pride, resentment and rivalry from their lives. Mark makes
clear in the chapters to follow that the disciples are not yet ready to
learn this lesson; only when they have been confronted with
Christ on the cross will they finally begin to learn the better way.

Reflect and pray

Confront us, dear Lord,
with all that holds us back
from following your way of grace and peace.

Confront us with our lack of understanding
of your costly cross and suffering love,
victorious over death itself.

Confront us with our false priorities
    and distorted comparisons,
our arguments over who is greater.

Confront us with our unwillingness
to see the good others do,
the generous acts by people
who are different to ourselves.

Confront us with all that makes us stumble,
all that builds a false kingdom,
not of your making.

Show us again your cross and empty tomb,
there to bring life abundantly.
Show us the child, any child,
your representative here on earth,
there to be welcomed joyfully.
Show us the cup of water,
there to be given generously
and received thankfully.

25 The welcoming one

Read Mark 10:1–16.

> 'Truly I tell you, whoever does not receive the kingdom of God like a little child will never enter it.' (Mark 10:15)

These two stories uphold the dignity and worth of women and children in opposition to the prevailing culture of Jesus' times. The first story explores the custom by which a husband could simply write a certificate of dismissal and divorce his wife. Jesus responds by speaking of this ruling as a reflection of hard hearts. Women are not chattels to be taken, used and then disposed of. Rather, Jesus stresses, they are equal human beings made in the image of God; from the beginning of creation 'God made them male and female' (10:6). He goes on to speak of the physical union of a man and woman as a God-given action, and one not to be set aside lightly. While Matthew and interpreters of our own times soften the teaching given – no doubt with good reason – Mark holds to the challenging ideal of marriage for life, seeing men and women as fundamentally equal in the relationship, by reason of God's actions and their own responsibility. For those who have experienced the breakdown of marriage, praying with this passage may be painful, but perhaps out of it all can hear the word that each of us is made in God's image and made in relationship.

The story of the blessing of the children has been the subject of numerous sentimental pictures; a blond-haired Jesus surrounded by children of all nations comes to mind. However, such distortions should not prevent us from seeing its central importance, for indeed the story goes close to the heart of Jesus' message of the kingdom. God's kingdom is not for us to build or achieve, but to receive, to receive openly and gladly like a child, and enter into. The rule of God comes not as a human project (God forbid!), but as a grace and blessing for us to receive and live out.

Reflect and pray

Blessed be our God,
the Creator who formed humanity,
male and female in the divine image.

Blessed be our God,
the saviour who welcomes each child
and enfolds humanity in the divine blessing.

Blessed be our God,
the Spirit who draws humanity together,
joining those once separate in the divine community.

Blessed be our God,
the Trinity – Creator, Saviour and Spirit –
there at the beginning of all things,
there at the heart of all life,
there at the fulfilment of the divine kingdom.

26 How shall I respond?

Read Mark 10:17–31.

> *Jesus, looking at him, loved him and said, 'You lack one thing ...'*
> (Mark 10:23)

Having told his followers that they must become like children to enter the kingdom, Jesus then meets a man who has grown up, grown complacent – having kept all the commandments since childhood (10:20) – and grown rich: 'he had many possessions' (10:22). He has also grown careless with his thinking and speaking. Jesus challenges the opening flattering address – the words 'Good Teacher' – with a cutting theological analysis. 'Why do you call me good? No one is good but God alone' (10:39). Mark is again using irony, for the rich man is meeting not simply a good teacher (words glibly said), but the goodness and love of God, seen in the face of Jesus Christ. Unfortunately he is too bound up with himself – his own achievements, possessions and concerns – to notice the fact.

Jesus accepts the man's question, 'What must I do to inherit eternal life?', despite it being rather individualistic and self-centred compared to Jesus' own focus on entering the kingdom. He answers it by pointing to the covenant and the commandments, quoting loosely six of the Ten Commandments. 'You shall not covet' becomes 'You shall not defraud', perhaps because a key element of this story is money.

The complacent man has done all these things, kept them and still feels restless. He asks for more, and this leads to Jesus' invitation to come and follow him. Despite Jesus' time and teaching, challenge and care, love and invitation, the man does not respond. He wants to know the answer and he wants to respond, but his possessions get in the way and he goes home sad. We are free to respond, free to choose, though as life proceeds we often become more and more bound up with ourselves, our achievements and our failures. The rich man has become like a camel trying to get through the eye of a needle – he does not fit. Instead he needs to learn from the blind beggar, named Bartimaeus (10:46), who, with nothing to lose, simply cries out to Jesus, 'Have mercy', is given new sight and then follows Jesus on the Way.

Reflect and pray

How shall I respond
  to your invitation
    to look again at life?
How shall I respond
  to your call
    to live the right way?
How shall I respond
  to your look
    of love for me?
How shall I respond
  to your challenge
    to let go of those things that possess me?
How shall I respond
  to your demand
    to reach out to the poor?
How shall I respond
  to your beckoning
    to follow you,
      here and now, whatever my life may be?
How shall I respond
  to my freedom
    to walk with you or to turn back?
How shall I respond?

27 Servant

Read Mark 10:32–45.

> *'But it shall not be so among you: but whoever wishes to be great among you must be your servant. (Mark 10:42)*

On its first reading to Mark's church community, this story of the request by the sons of thunder must have caused some controversy, with its focus on radical service. Those in his church who were 'lording it over' the others, or who wanted to do so, would have had burning ears as they heard Jesus' firm words: 'It shall not be so among you.' When Matthew came to retell the story he was sufficiently embarrassed on behalf of John and James to place the request on their mother's lips (Matthew 20:20); after all, what wouldn't a mother do for her sons?

The passage has much in common with the teaching of the second chapter of Philippians, where Paul focuses on the *kenosis* – the self-emptying of Christ on the cross.

Paul wrote:

> Let the same mind be in you that was in Christ Jesus,
> > who, though he was in the form of God,
> > > did not regard equality with God
> > > as something to be exploited,
> > but emptied himself,
> > > taking the form of a slave. (Philippians 2:5–7a)

Scholars see Paul as quoting from an early Christian hymn, either of his own writing or in circulation among the churches. It may have been a hymn that in time was sung in Mark's own church community. Jesus challenges the grasping after or exploitation of position – the lording over – and speaks instead of the way of service and self-giving. In fact he takes this idea further, moving from the *diakonos*, servant, of the earlier passage (9:35 and 10:43) to *doulos*, slave (10:44).

The slave was owned and ruled by his or her master, 'the ultimate expression of powerlessness',[62] and it is this picture Jesus uses here to describe what he is about – the Lord who is the slave, emptying himself, giving himself as a ransom payment to free 'the many'. Here is Jesus' upside-down kingdom: Jesus is Lord, who is slave to all; Jesus is the Messiah, but one who suffers. The influence of the book of Isaiah – and in particular the servant songs of Isaiah 42—53 – is seen again on Jesus and the community founded in his name. For those in Mark's church (and our own) who wish to ape the ways of the Roman Empire, with absolute power, strict control and rigid hierarchy, this is a hard lesson to hear, but it is the way of Jesus, our slave-of-all Lord.

Reflect and pray

Where we use our faith for our own selfish ends,
seeking the best seats in heaven,
    Lord Jesus, speak your word of authority:
    'It shall not be so among you.'
Where we play the power game,
making comparisons with others,
sensing our own superiority,
    Lord Jesus, speak your word of authority:
    'It shall not be so among you.'
Where we build hierarchies,
looking to others to lead and direct,
forgetting the way of service,
    Lord Jesus, speak your word of authority:
    'It shall not be so among you.'
Where we forget the cost of discipleship,
the letting go of baptism,
the drinking of the cup,
the way of the cross,
    Lord Jesus, speak your word of authority:
    'It shall not be so among you.'

Lord Jesus, show us the servant way.
Renew your Church
to be a people where there is no lording over others,
no 'us' and 'them',
no best and worst seats,
but one body
baptised in you,
fed by you,
sharing your cup of blessing with the world.

28 Blessed is the One

Read Mark 10:46—11:11.

> *They shouted: 'Hosanna! Blessed is the one who comes in the name of the Lord!' (Mark 11:9)*

Once more Mark introduces a key story (and new stage in his narrative) with a miracle of sight being restored. With typical irony Bartimaeus the blind beggar has greater insight into who Jesus is than many of his sighted companions, as he calls out: 'Jesus, Son of David, have mercy on me!' Bartimaeus effectively becomes an example to Mark's hearers of true discipleship or as Joel Marcus describes it 'a symbol of the new disciple'.[63] He persistently cries out to Jesus, despite the attempts by the crowd to silence him. His persistence is rewarded by Jesus stopping still (a remarkable moment in the urgent journey that has propelled him forward from Galilee to Jerusalem to meet his hour). He hears Jesus' call, passed on to him by others, 'Take heart, get up, he is calling you', and responds with urgent joy. He throws off his cloak, as the pilgrims will later throw their cloaks down before Jesus when he enters the city and as new Christians in Mark's community will do as they prepare for baptism. Jesus asks the key question: 'What do you want me to do for you?' Here is a dialogue where Bartimaeus is given a voice, to voice his deepest longings, rather than to be silenced. His answer to Jesus, 'My teacher let me see again', expresses his total faith and trust in Jesus and in itself brings restoration. Now seeing anew he follows Jesus 'on the way'.

The way (an early name for Christians being followers of the way) is the way to Jerusalem, the way to the cross and beyond, and Jesus provides a sign of what he is about by riding into Jerusalem on a colt to the delight of the pilgrims that follow. Bartimaeus' story has prepared the way for a new stage of the gospel, as Jesus is recognised as the Davidic Messiah, the Son of David, and makes his claim over city and temple by riding through its gates on a young donkey.

Reflect and pray

Jesus, friend of blind beggars,
we rejoice in your coming
and offer you our cries for help and our shouts of triumph.
With your fallible followers of every age,
we pray 'have mercy'
and sing 'Hosanna! Hosanna in highest heaven!'

You ride a young donkey,
mocking our delusions of grandeur and grasps of power.
You are no ordinary king.
No King David, using power for selfish ends.
No King Herod, mixing weakness with tyranny.
No Caesar, with worldly empire grounded in violence.
You do not lord it over your subjects,
but come in humble life-giving glory.
Your kingdom breaks into our world and into our lives,
as vision is restored, hope is made real, joy bursts out,
    peace is given a chance.

Hosanna! Blessed are you, Lord Jesus.
Blessed is your kingdom!
Blessed is the promise you bring to our troubled world.
Hosanna in highest heaven!

29 House of prayer

Read Mark 11:12–25.

> *He was teaching and saying, 'Is it not written, "My house shall be called a house of prayer for all nations." But you have made it a den of robbers.' (Mark 11:17)*

Mark began the gospel with words from Malachi and Isaiah, speaking of one preparing the nation for the coming of the Lord. Now Jesus comes to the temple and confronts it with the universal vision of Isaiah – the temple called to be a house of prayer for all nations and the people a light to the nations.

Mark, as so often, weaves stories together to underline their meaning and in this passage Jesus' clearing of the temple is wrapped in the strange story of the barren fig tree. Whatever the roots of this story – whether in incident or parable – Mark sees it in symbolic terms as a prophetic word against the corrupt temple. The fig tree was used many times in the Old Testament as a picture of the nation or temple and its fruit or lack of it. In the years leading up to the invasion of Israel and destruction of the first temple, the prophet Jeremiah spoke of God's judgement on his own nation in this way: 'When I wanted to gather them, says the Lord, there are no grapes on the vine, nor figs on the fig tree' (Jeremiah 8:13a). Hosea and Micah make similar references to the fig tree (Hosea 2:12; Micah 7:1), again describing the lack of the fruit and the resulting destruction of the tree.

The shift from the barren fig tree to the teaching on prayer seems at first sight a confusing one and has led some to see the effective cursing of the fig tree as a small example of moving mountains and praying with faith. However, Mark's focus has been on the temple and its calling to be a house of prayer to all nations.

With the temple having failed in that calling – a fruitless fig tree that is heading towards destruction – Jesus now calls his disciples to take up that ministry of prayer.

Fundamental to that prayer is trust in God. As Frances Young wrote movingly in her book *Face to Face* (a book about life with her severely disabled son Arthur): 'Faith is accepting what God has done, and trusting him for all that is to come. Faith is not desperately trying to believe six impossible things before breakfast.'[64] This trust is not about manipulating reality, but it is about placing the whole of life before God with open hands, to the point that it is as if God has already answered one's cry. Such prayer in Mark's eyes opens up immense possibilities, but it is not a power to be misused. Immediately Jesus links this praying in faith with forgiveness, for resentment and anger against others becomes a block to God's work in and through us.

Reflect and pray

Build a house of prayer, Lord Jesus,
a home not of stones or sacred places,
but made of your people,
your followers of every time and place.

Build a house of prayer, Lord Jesus,
and make me a living stone
within that temple,
centred and dependent on others and on you.

Build a house of prayer, Lord Jesus,
open to all nations, all peoples, all faiths and none.
all seekers after truth and life.

Build a house of prayer, Lord Jesus,
free from corruption or hypocrisy, hatred or fear,
renewed each moment by your Spirit.

Build a house of prayer, Lord Jesus,
a mighty tree that bears fruit in every season,
in faith and forgiveness,
in word and deed.

30 Tenants

Read Mark 11:27—12:12.

'A man planted a vineyard ... and leased it to tenants.'
(Mark 12:1)

Having spent the evening outside the city, Jesus returns to the city and the temple. He has spoken his word of challenge and judgement over the temple, seeing it as a fig tree that has become barren, a house of prayer for all turned into a den for robbers. Now he enters into a debate with his opponents, which begins with his authority being questioned. 'By what authority are you doing these things?', the religious leaders ask (11:28). This has been a key question from the very beginning of the gospel and Mark has no doubt about the answer to the question. John the Baptist had recognised Jesus' authority (1:7) and the crowd had done so too (1:22). His teaching (1:27) and his actions (2:10) had shown that his authority had come from God.

Jesus refuses to answer the question and instead refers back to John the Baptist – the first witness to the divine authorisation of Jesus; there, as John baptised Jesus, the divine voice had spoken from heaven: 'You are my Son, the Beloved; with you I am well pleased' (1:11). Now Jesus asks the leaders: 'Did the baptism of John come from heaven or was it of human origin?' (11:30). Their failure to answer shows their inability to recognise who is standing before them. And so the debate continues and other questions are asked. But before moving to these, Mark slips in a parable to drive home the failure of the leaders to listen to the voice from heaven and to welcome Jesus.

It is a grim story of tenants at odds with the vineyard owner – a parable not only for the situation in first-century Palestine, but for our own times too. What kind of tenants are we in God's vineyard?

Reflect and pray

Remind us, God of the beloved,
that we are only tenants, not the owners:
  Not the owners of our children,
    for they must grow to become themselves.
  Not the owners of our homes,
  for they must be places of welcome and friendship.
  Not the owners of the Church,
  for the Church must be yours, called to your work.
  Not the owners of our nation,
  for there is but one humanity
    and we are part of each other.
  Not the owners of this planet,
  for earth is your place, created for all your creatures.
Challenge our attempts to seize control,
to satisfy our selfish greed,
to grasp what we consider our inheritance.

Make us willing to receive your prophets of today,
uncomfortable, unexpected voices
that remind us that all is on loan
and all is to be respected.

And show us your beloved Son
who does not grasp his inheritance,
but offers his life for friend and enemy alike,
for the sake of the vineyard, the earth, the kingdom.

31 Death and taxes

Read Mark 12:13–27.

Jesus said to them, 'Is not this the reason you are wrong, that you know neither the scriptures nor the power of God?' (Mark 12:24)

As Benjamin Franklin famously said, 'In this world nothing is certain but death and taxes.'[65] Two of the great debates of history are played out in this pair of stories of the questions directed at Jesus in his final days in Jerusalem. This pair is placed within a setting of five key questions about authority, taxes, resurrection, the greatest commandment and the nature of the Messiah. The first three questions are asked by Jesus' opponents – the chief priests, the Pharisees and the Sadducees – while the fourth comes from an unexpected ally impressed by the nature of Jesus' answers, and the fifth is raised by Jesus himself.

The questions emphasise the value of debate within Mark's community; he and his fellow Christians expect to be able to give account for the hope that is within them (1 Peter 3:15). They are not frightened of argument, neither within the church community nor in response to the questions and challenges of non-Christians of all backgrounds.

Here in the face of these two great questions, Jesus responds with a powerful vision of God. Caesar may have his place, but there is no question that responsibility to the state is placed in the bigger context of responsibility to God – the God who is beyond all national boundaries and all ethnic divisions. In a myriad of ways, whether outwardly religious or not, prisoners of conscience have witnessed to the truth that all rulers are answerable to a greater authority.

Equally, the Sadducees' trick question – and their mocking story of the woman with seven husbands – is confronted with the vision of the God who is beyond time and in whose eyes the great heroes of the faith are alive. It is a perfect rebuff to the Sadducees to whom Abraham, Isaac and Jacob are so important.

Reflect and pray

God of demanding justice,
we hold before you the emperors of our day:
   those who hold the power of government,
   those authorised by the vote of the people,
   and those who have grasped power by fear
     or violence or corruption;
   those who exercise their influence with wisdom
    and compassion
   and those whose tyranny is cruel and self-serving.

They have their time,
but YOUR TIME will come.
Confront them with your judgement and mercy.
Expose the wrong and reveal your piercing truth
  and self-giving way.

God of overflowing life,
we hold before you all who have died:
   those who trusted you to the end;
   those who were bewildered and afraid;
   those who cursed you and the night;
   those who hoped for nothing.

They had their time,
but YOUR TIME is greater.
You are the Lord of life,
the God of the living.
Look with mercy on all your creation, all your children.
With Abraham, Isaac and Jacob,
with Moses and Miriam and Elijah,
with Mary and Peter and Mark,
bring us to the glory of your presence,
where, like angels, all sound out your praise
in joy and gladness, light and peace,
through Jesus Christ, the mighty Saviour and risen Lord.

32 *The good scribe*

Read Mark 12:28–44.

When Jesus saw that he answered wisely, he said to him, 'You are not far from the kingdom of God.' (Mark 12:34)

So far in the great temple debate, Jesus' opponents have played true to form, with the elders questioning his authority (11:27, 28), the Pharisees and Herodians trying to trick him over taxes, and the Sadducees mocking belief in the resurrection. Each fulfils the stereotype of an opponent. But Mark is happy to break the stereotypes he has constructed, to show that anyone – whatever their party or background – can respond positively to Jesus. The scribe hears how well Jesus answers and brings his own sincerely felt question.

Jesus' answer – like that he gave to the rich man – is rooted in the Hebrew Scriptures and the Jewish story. It instinctively begins with the great Shema 'Hear O Israel' – an affirmation used at the beginning and end of the day – and then links this with love for neighbour, a piece of religious brilliance. Jesus 'is not saying anything startlingly novel',[66] as this link had already been made in Judaism. In fact, Luke in his retelling of Mark's story is quite content to place the linked commandments on the lips of the scribe and for Jesus to respond by explaining the meaning of 'neighbour'. However, whatever the history of this twin commandment that is in effect one command, it is the essence of Jesus' Way.

The scribe's recognition of this makes him in Jesus' words 'not far from the kingdom'. In a classic piece of listening, the scribe reflects back what Jesus has said to him, repeating it phrase by phrase and making it his own. This is the kind of attentive listening God asks of Jesus' followers on the mountain of transfiguration. To be 'not far from the kingdom' is to listen to Jesus, and to learn from him a new depth and breadth of loving.

Reflect and pray

May we learn, Lord Jesus,
from the good scribe
who echoes your words
and sees how love for God
and neighbour outweighs
all ritual and sacrifices.
   Deepen our love.

May we learn, Lord,
from the crowd
who delights to listen to you,
as you put King David in his place
and show yourself as the surprising Messiah.
   Open our hearts.

May we learn, Lord,
from the corrupted scribes
whose lives are all show with no substance,
exposed by you
for their longing for respect,
their disregard for the needy,
their long prayers that do not connect
with God or with life.
   Guard us from evil.

May we learn, Lord,
from the widow
whose two small coins speak of sacrifice and grace
and point to your self-giving love
offered on a cross.
   Show us your way.

33 Alert and awake

Read Mark 13.

'And what I say to you I say to all: Keep awake.' (*Mark 13:37*)

With chapter 13 we enter the world of apocalyptic literature – writings about the end times. This way of looking at the world had grown up in Judaism after the Exile as a response to the sufferings of God's people and the chaotic events occurring around them; examples of this form can be found in the books of Ezekiel and Daniel. In the early Church it found its greatest expression in the Revelation of John with its dramatic depiction of heaven and the final struggle between good and evil.

The early Christians saw themselves as living in end times and expected the culmination of history (and Christ's return) initially within their generation. Jesus' own words seem to imply this: 'Truly I tell you, this generation will not pass away until all these things have taken place' (13:30).

However, even in the early Church, there was increasing recognition that the end was not in their control or knowledge, and so Mark includes Jesus saying: 'But about that day or hour no one knows, neither the angels in heaven, nor the Son, but only the Father' (13:32). History is littered with eccentric predictions of the End, which have passed by without incident, and Mark will have none of it.

Alongside the cataclysmic events the chapter speaks of is the expectation that the followers of Jesus will be persecuted and this was a reality that the young Church experienced all too soon. As Elizabeth Struthers Malbon points out, there are two passions described in the gospel: 'The Gospel of Mark has, as it were, a double ending: the passion of Jesus (chapters 14—16) and the passion of the community (chapter 13).'[67] The cross that Mark's hearers are called to bear may not simply be a symbol of self-denial and self-giving, but a very real cross of martyrdom. In this, the early Church has been followed by Christians of every century who have given the ultimate price for their faith.

In all these dark sayings two key commands stand out: first, the call to rely on the Holy Spirit's help (13:11), giving us the words we need and the courage to say them; second, the need to be alert (13:23, 33, 35, 37) and to pray (13:18).

Reflect and pray

We are anxious, Lord of our times,
anxious for ourselves, our children
    and our children's children.
There are such fearsome signs of disturbance
in the life of humanity and of the planet itself:
nations torn apart by ethnic and religious hatred,
the bitter scars of outrage followed by outrage;
the divide of rich and poor
reaching to an unbridgeable chasm,
set to explode.
We are anxious about a faith on the defensive,
facing deadly persecution in so many nations
and mockery in our own.
We worry for the planet's sake,
groaning under the heat of our consumption
and the weight of our numbers.
False prophets come proclaiming your greatness,
    yet living a lie.
Would-be messiahs peddle beguiling answers
    that do not match reality.
Fear gathers yet more fear.

Where are we to turn?

Come, Holy Spirit,
give us new words to speak,
to bring hope to your world.

Come, Holy Spirit,
wake us up to the cries of our planet.

Come, Holy Spirit,
make us watchful for signs of the kingdom
breaking into the life of this world.

Come, Holy Spirit,
open our ears to the words of Christ,
the words which will never pass away.

Come, Holy Spirit,
give us the wisdom to discern uncomfortable truths
and to turn from all that is false.

34 Remember her

Read Mark 14:1–11.

> 'Truly I tell you, wherever the good news is proclaimed in the whole world, what she has done will be told in remembrance of her.'
> (*Mark 14:9*)

As so often Mark interweaves two stories here to bring out their dramatic contrast and interconnection. The plot to kill Jesus (and the involvement of one of the twelve, Judas, in this) is broken in two to allow Mark to tell the story of the unnamed and unknown woman who anoints Jesus for the task ahead.

Here is the new Davidic king, the Messiah, the Son of God, being anointed not in the temple but in a leper's house, not by the chief priest but by an unnamed woman. The king's anointing will lead on to the enthronement of the cross where Jesus will wear the crown of thorns and be charged with being 'the King of the Jews'. The breaking of the jar and the 'waste' of the costly perfume both point to the costly, seemingly wasteful action of Jesus in his dying, and prepare his body for burial. In that sense it is a sacramental action, a physical sign pointing beyond itself.

Beginning with the solemn 'Amen' – 'Truly I tell you' – Jesus informs his disciples that wherever the good news is preached, what the woman has done will be told in remembrance of her. It is a glorious affirmation of the witness and ministry of women – and this particular unnamed woman – in the Church, yet sadly over the centuries those words of Jesus have often been forgotten or ignored. The waste of the perfume and the loss of Jesus' life lead on to good news being proclaimed in the whole world, a triumphal resurrection promise in the darkest of moments.

As Joan Mitchell comments:

Small wonder that her action should be proclaimed: it summarises the good news ... Her prophetic action reaches to the end of the story, where Jesus whom she anointed as king does not need to be anointed for death, because he is no longer in the tomb. Proclaiming the woman's action proclaims Jesus' messianic identity – the good news.[68]

Reflect and pray

So it begins
the plot, the planned arrest under cover of darkness,
the scheme to silence this Jesus.
Money passes hands
and one who listened to his words and shared his food,
one who walked the dusty roads of Palestine in his
company,
one whom he loves,
seeks now to betray him.

And in the midst of this darkness
  an unnamed woman,
  a jar of precious perfume,
  an action that speaks of a Messiah,
  and a burial.

God, in whose image we are made, female and male,
may this woman remind us of
  all women who give costly service,
  all women who experience the anger of angry men,
  all women who are noticed and affirmed by Jesus,
  all women who are caught up in the plots of the
    powerful,
  all women who play their part in your good news story,
    your overwhelming, costly, gracious act of love.

35 New in the kingdom of God

Read Mark 14:12–25.

> *'Truly I tell you, I will never again drink of the fruit of the vine until
> that day when I drink it new in the kingdom of God.' (Mark 14:25)*

A eucharistic theme has flowed through the gospel, with Jesus
having twice taken bread and given thanks at the feeding of the
five thousand (6:41) and four thousand (8:6). He has eaten with his
friends at Simon and Andrew's home (1:29) and at Levi's (2:15).
Now he gathers his disciples in an upper room to share a last
supper with them. This is no simple fellowship meal; it is the
Passover meal, part of the week-long feast of the Unleavened
Bread, the great Jewish celebration of the terrible and awesome
events surrounding the liberation of Israel from slavery in Egypt. It
is an act of remembrance that involves the sacrifice of a lamb, the
sharing of a meal, the recounting of a story and the singing of the
great Passover hymns (Psalms 115–118).

Now Jesus connects those events of liberation and sacrifice to
his own death. As he did with the loaves and fishes shared with the
crowds, he takes the bread and wine and gives thanks to God,
using the traditional Jewish blessing for each: 'Blessed are you, O
Lord our God, king of the universe, who brings forth bread from
the earth', for the bread, and, with similar words, 'Blessed are you,
O Lord our God, king of the universe, who creates the fruit of the
vine', for the wine. The focus of his prayer of blessing and
thanksgiving is not so much the bread or wine as the God who
gave them and whose will and kingdom are his raison d'être.

His words to the disciples and invitation to take, eat and drink
draw them into his action which is for them and for 'many'
(referred to here at 14:24 and previously at 10:45). Jesus' death is
not for the few – the correct, the righteous, the inner circle – but
for the many – the tax collectors and sinners, the fallible disciples

and the ordinary crowd. This 'many' focus must challenge our
narrow interpretations of who should be invited to share in the
meal. In bread and wine we remember once more what Christ has
done, not simply for us but for the world.

Reflect and pray

God beyond time, beyond space,
we thank you for that moment in history
in a room hidden in Jerusalem
when Jesus took the bread which friends had prepared.

We thank you for the hands
tense with all that was to come,
lifting the bread, holding it there before them.

We thank you for the words he spoke,
forgetting the betrayal around him,
focusing all his soul in blessing you,
thanking you for all you gave and give.

We thank you for the breaking,
hands tearing the loaf apart,
crumbs flying, eyes watching,
caught up in the drama of pain and sacrifice.

We thank you for the giving
to each of those frail disciples;
the insistent words he used,
'Take it, this is my body.'

We thank you for the cup,
the words of thanks again,
the offering for all,
his blood poured out not for a few but for many,
the taste of the kingdom to come.

We thank you for that fleeting moment
grounded in time,
held in the confines of a crowded room,
yet resounding down the centuries to touch our lives today,
to feed and refresh us,
to show us your kingdom.

Help us to take what Christ has given,
to bless and thank you,
as he did so long ago.

36 The cup

Read Mark 14:26–52.

'Abba Father, for you all things are possible; remove this cup from me; yet, not what I want, but what you want.' (Mark 14:36)

Here at Gethsemane we reach the pinnacle of prayer in the gospel. The dark shadow of betrayal and death lengthens as Jesus and his disciples move from the safety of the upper room to the vulnerability of the garden. Having reached the garden, Jesus draws to one side with his three closest companions – Simon, John and James – those who had been with him at the bedside of Jairus' dead daughter and on the mountaintop of glorious vision.

Jesus confronts the awesome and awe-full nature of what he is to do and is to be done to him and he is overwhelmed with sorrow. Throwing himself on the ground he prays to his God with the word that expresses utter trust and love – Abba. His belief is total, but it is not enough to move the mountain that he faces. Faith bows to a greater reality – the will of God – not as some predetermined fate or stoical necessity, but the work of God's love in this broken world. 'If I have all faith, so as to remove mountains, but do not have love, I am nothing' (1 Corinthians 13:2). Jesus asks for the cup to be removed, for this cup is none other than the 'cup of destruction' (Ezekiel 23:33), 'the cup of calamity, the cup of wrath' (Isaiah 51:17). It is the pouring out of his life, his very self, of which he has spoken on the way and in the upper room.

There is no breaking of the cloud, no removal of the cup of wrath. The God who revealed himself at the baptism and the mountaintop does not appear or speak, but his prayer enables Jesus to know that Abba has heard and the work ahead is Abba's will for his creation. The disciples stand by, exhausted, helpless and useless; their strength has gone – now they can only look to Jesus to drink the cup on their behalf.

Reflect on the cup Jesus is to drink

The cup is there before us,
the mocking cup,
full of the dregs of human suffering,
full of the bitter cruelty,
full of the cheap injustice,
full of the sad sin of the world.

The cup is there and none will drink it.
None place their lips on its deadly rim.

We close our eyes;
we look away;
we pray to the God who seems silent.

And one walks forward
alone
and takes the cup
alone
and hesitates
alone.
'Abba remove this cup from me,'
he prays,
alone.
'Yet not what I want,
but what you want.'
Alone
he prays to the God who seems silent.
And slowly, painfully,
he takes the cup
and drains it to its very depths
alone,
risking his all for this world,
loving his all for our sake's,
placing his all in the hands
of the God who seems silent.

A footnote to the young disciple's desertion of Jesus

A certain young man was following him, wearing nothing but a linen cloth. They caught hold of him, but he left the linen cloth and ran off naked. (Mark 14:51)

One tradition has it that this is an autobiographical note; that Mark was the young man who fled naked from the scene of Jesus' arrest. Attractive though this may be, there is no evidence to support the idea and it does not fit in with present-day thinking about the formation of the gospel. A more recent way of reflecting on the verse is that it is highly symbolic, reflecting an image of baptism: the naked man of this verse is balanced by the young man clothed in white at the tomb. The picture would connect with the practice of baptism in the early Church and Paul's image of baptism as a re-clothing: 'you have stripped off the old self with its practices and have clothed yourself with the new self' (Colossians 3:9). Again this may be reading too much into a verse which as likely as not is simply a description of the kind of panic that gripped Jesus' followers at that moment in the garden, as dreams were shattered – what C. H. Dodd describes as 'a bare matter of fact'![69] As we read the one-verse story, fact and symbolism intertwine; the sense of crisis is heightened by the echo of prophetic words – 'and those of stout heart among the mighty shall flee away naked in that day, says the Lord' (Amos 2:16). As Augustus Toplady would write many centuries later:

> Nothing in my hand I bring;
> Simply to the cross I cling;
> Naked, come to thee for dress
> Helpless look to thee for grace.[70]

Reflect on the image of the naked young man fleeing

The last scrap
of pious pretension
slips from my shoulders
as violent hands
reach out to hold me.

I run, glad at first to be free.
But then comes the shame.
Like Adam and Eve,
all I desire is to hide
my nakedness
from others and from God.

Darkness covers me,
yet God sees to the heart:
darkness and light
are the same to the One
who formed me
and the One who now
stripped of all but love
hangs on a cross
amid daytime darkness
to free me and many.

37 Tears

Read Mark 14:53–72.

Then Peter remembered that Jesus had said to him, 'Before the cock crows twice, you will deny me three times.' And he broke down and wept. (Mark 14:72)

One of the key characters in Mark's gospel is Simon Peter; in fact, after Jesus he is by far the most mentioned figure in the story, being introduced in the first chapter with the call of the disciples (1:16) and referred to by name in the final message of Jesus after the resurrection, 'tell his disciples *and Peter*' (16:7). Between those two references come twenty-two references by name to Simon, renamed Peter by Jesus in 3:16; it is small wonder that the tradition grew in the Church that Mark's gospel owed its content to the reminiscences of Peter.

In the story, Peter shows insight and courage, leaving all to follow Jesus and being the first to declare Jesus to be the Messiah; he is privileged to be part of the inner circle that sees Jesus glorified on the mount of transfiguration. However, he shares with the other disciples their many misunderstandings and mistakes and is identified with the ways of Satan when he tries to stop Jesus speaking of the cross as his destiny (8:33). While having the courage to follow at a distance after Jesus' arrest, he denies knowledge of Jesus at the crucial moment of testing. His very fallibility has, of course, made him an example that has inspired fallible followers of every generation. He is what Elizabeth Struthers Malbon describes as a 'round character' (following the work of E. M. Forster) and 'round characters elicit identification in a way that flat characters do not'.[71]

Peter fails his Lord at the crucial moment by following only at a safe distance, unwilling to risk himself and openly declare his loyalty to Jesus in the great test: a challenge to Mark's readers who may face danger in their own professing of Christian faith. However, as Peter hears the cock crow he remembers the words of Jesus – the task Mark is setting all his readers – and he weeps, a prayer in itself that seeks the mercy of God.

Reflect and pray

Here is Peter's prayer.
Not the following at a safe distance,
watching from the sidelines
the death-trap closing on Jesus.
Not the hasty words of denial,
the pretence of innocence,
the curses and the oaths:
'I do not know this man.'

Here is Peter's prayer:
the sound of dawn
breaking into his mind,
making him to remember
the words of his Lord and Teacher, the Galilean Jesus,
the breaking down and flowing tears.

There is Peter's prayer – in tears and brokenness.
So, dear God, we hold before you all
   who shed bitter tears today:
   tears over relationships destroyed,
   trust broken, faith denied.
May their hot and bitter tears be for you
   a prayer of brokenness,
that healing and forgiveness may flow once more
   and new beginnings come where all was lost.
We ask in the name of our Lord and Teacher,
   the Galilean Jesus.

38 Handed over

Read Mark 15:1–20.

> *They bound Jesus, led him away and handed him over to Pilate.*
> *(Mark 15:1)*

Having dominated the pages of the gospel by his wise words and mighty deeds Jesus now becomes a passive figure – done to, rather than doing. He turns from subject to object – bound, led, handed over and questioned. Before Pilate's questioning Jesus remains silent and gives no reply. Yet for Mark the divine glory shines through Jesus in a new and even more profound way. Pilate's amazement is not simply confusion and puzzlement, but a sign that God is at work, echoing all the other times Jesus has caused awe and wonder among those he has met. Vanstone describes this as a kind of waiting, receiving and exposure to the world and concludes: 'as he does so, a figure exposed and waiting, he appears no diminished or degraded figure but a figure of enormous dignity.'[72]

Here is one of Mark's paradoxes: the one who apparently has the power – Pilate the governor whose word can bring life or death – is shown to be confused and weak before the bound silent prisoner – Jesus who is to die to bring life. There is mocking irony throughout Mark's telling of the story. Repeatedly the charge is hurled at Jesus that he has claimed to be 'King of the Jews' (the phrase is used four times in this passage) and the soldiers take this a step further by dressing Jesus in purple, crowning him with a garland of thorns and saluting him. Each act of cruelty and brutality degrades those involved rather than the prisoner – the power of the temple, the Roman Empire and the mob are each exposed to the thorn-crowned king and found wanting.

Reflect and pray

We stand in solidarity with all who have been handed over.
Handed over to be tried unjustly,
    to be tortured and mocked.
Handed over to be done to,
dehumanised,
stripped and beaten,
reduced to mere flesh.

  May their cries be heard in the corners of heaven.
We stand in solidarity with all who have been handed over
to the will of the mob,
the whim of the powerful,
the plotting of those who know best.

  May their cries shake our world into newness.
We stand in solidarity with Jesus, the thorn-crowned king
as he stands before Pilate, the emperor's representative,
and amazes him with his stunning silence,
as he absorbs the chief priests' hatred
and satisfies the bloodlust of the crowd,
as he wears the mocking cloak and receives the lashes,
    spit and laughter.

We kneel in homage of our thorn-crowned king
not in mockery, please God, but
in awe and wonder,
grief and hope,
determination to rid the world
of the torturers' tools and the powers that bind and destroy
and to follow this Jesus wherever he leads.

39 The body broken and curtain torn

Read Mark 15:21–47.

> *Then Jesus gave a loud cry and breathed his last. And the curtain of the temple was torn in two, from top to bottom.* (Mark 15:37, 38)

So Mark's story comes to its climax, in the dying – or life-giving – of Jesus; this is where the narrative has been heading from the very beginning. In Mark's telling, the cross is rooted in history, but is also rich in symbolism – the two cannot be separated. The suffering of Christ is told with brutal realism – the stripping of Jesus, the mockery, the mental anguish of Jesus' cry, the last breath and the removal of the dead body. Yet interwoven into this portrayal are pointer after pointer to the meaning of what is happening, as Mark draws on the imagery of the psalms and brings out the irony of each element of the event. The customary notice giving the charge against the crucified becomes a proclamation of Jesus' kingship: 'The King of the Jews' (15:26). The mocking words of the passers-by point to the saving work that Jesus is accomplishing: 'He saved others; he cannot save himself' (15:31). The acclamation of the Roman centurion echoes the affirmation of Jesus by God at his baptism, when the voice from heaven calls out: 'You are my Son, my Beloved; with you I am well pleased' (1:11). Noting this, Ernest Best comments: 'Thus the story is held together at its beginning and end.'[73]

The story has come full circle and Jesus' baptism has been fulfilled. Just as the heavens were torn open then, so the temple curtain – the veil to the holy of holies – is now torn in two, from top to bottom, to reveal and release the presence and power of God. The Gentile centurion speaks the prophetic words that echo the divine voice: 'Truly this man was God's Son.' Far from being the point of defeat, Jesus' passion becomes, in Vanstone's words, 'the decisive manifestation of His divinity'.[74]

The women disciples watch in horror and awe, witnesses to the event which is turning the world upside down and revealing the torn heart of God.

Reflect and pray

Let us be still before the cross
    not in the company of the mockers,
    the passers-by who wag their heads and shout their
    jeers,
    the scribes and chief priests whose mocking cry rings
      down the centuries,
    'He saved others; he cannot save himself',
    the bandits who taunt and jeer in their pain,
    and all who look for a sign,
    a magic miracle, where Jesus jumps down from the cross
    or is helped down by Elijah and all is right with the
    world.

Let us be still before the cross
    in the company of the women
    who followed this carpenter of Nazareth
      and listened to his words,
    the centurion who reported the death and saw the truth,
    and that other Joseph who, waiting and longing
      for your kingdom,
    provided a final dignity to that death-torn body.

Let us be still before the cross
    and enter its mystery
    in the company of the God of Jesus
    who seems so far off, so absent
    and yet is there in the parting cry, the final breath,
      the torn curtain,
    death turned into release (for many),
    pain become a prayer (for the world),
    hatred met by love (for all).

40 He is not here, he is going ahead

Read Mark 16:1–8.

> *'But go, tell his disciples and Peter that he is going ahead of you to Galilee; there you will see him, just as he told you.'* (Mark 16:7)

The final chapter of Mark's gospel has caused many debates among scholars, given the varied endings that are found among early manuscripts of the gospels. It is generally recognised that verses beyond verse 8 are later additions, added to bring it to a neater and seemingly more satisfactory ending. The oldest manuscripts bring the gospel to an abrupt halt with the description of the women fleeing the tomb in terror and the closing words, 'they said nothing to anyone, for they were afraid'. In fact, the final word is 'for'. As Morna Hooker wryly comments: 'Grammarians are shocked all the way through by Mark's Greek.'[75] Many find this puzzling in the extreme and feel that the original ending to the gospel must have been lost or even that Mark was interrupted in his writing. However, others recognise that the abrupt ending has its own power, drawing the gospel to a close with a sense of awe and wonder at the action of God (a recurring theme in the gospel). Donald Juel suggests: 'Mark's Gospel forbids that closure. There is no stone at the mouth of the tomb. Jesus is out, on the same side of the door as the women and the readers.'[76] As so often, Mark is pointing beyond his own writing to a reality that cannot be contained within its pages. If the gospel was being read out in the setting of worship it would no doubt be followed by worship and prayer, which might include the celebration of the Lord's Supper reminding the hearers that indeed Christ was with them, as he had made himself known to those first disciples. The women among Mark's hearers would be able to tell how the first women followers had not remained silent for ever and indeed had passed on that message to Mark's own community that Jesus was not in the tomb but going ahead of them.

Almost two thousand years later we cannot look for evidence of bones present or absent from a tomb, nor know for certain what the women encountered on that day. But we can listen to Mark who like the young man at the tomb says to us: 'He is not here; he has gone ahead of you.' Jesus is not trapped by tomb or death, doctrine or scientific definition, but free to be met and followed in our own Galilees, always going before us.

Reflect and pray

Risen Jesus,
you stun me with your absence.
You cannot be entombed
in rock or stone,
in ecclesiastical structures
or scholarly debates,
scientific definition
or doctrinal niceties.

You cannot be bound
by Satan's powers
or human evils.
You are the Strong One
who turns the tables
on death itself and all wickedness.

I have followed you through this gospel's pages
but you are not trapped within its words.
You walk free,
beyond its letters,
beyond its control.
You are not in this book,
but let loose
on an unsuspecting world.
You are no tame lion.

You cannot be grasped or controlled,
only followed,
   met in the Galilees of the workmen and the wounded,
   the frail and the fallible;
   met among the ordinary
   children, women and men;
   met in the towns and cities,
     hills and valleys of the here and now.
Glory to you, dear Teacher.
Glory to you, the Servant One.
Glory to you, my risen Lord,
here and now and for ever. Amen.

Notes

1   Martin Luther King Jr, source unknown.

2   Wendy Beckett, *The Gaze of Love* (London: Marshall Pickering, 1993), p. 9.

3   Stephen C. Barton, *The Spirituality of the Gospels* (London: SPCK, 1992), p. 146.

4   Michael Mayne, *The Enduring Melody* (London: Darton, Longman & Todd, 2006), p. 10.

5   Christopher Burdon, *Stumbling on God: Faith and Vision in Mark's Gospel* (Grand Rapids MI: Eerdmans, 1990), p. 8.

6   Walter Brueggemann, *Great Prayers of the Old Testament* (Louisville KY: Westminster John Knox Press, 2008), p. xxviii.

7   Benignus O'Rourke, *Finding Your Hidden Treasure* (Darton, Longman & Todd, 2010), p. 11.

8   Eugene Peterson, *Eat this Book: A Conversation in the Art of Spiritual Reading* (London: Hodder & Stoughton, 2006), p. 85.

9   David Foster OSB, *Reading with God* (London: Continuum, 2005), p. 14.

10 Foster OSB, *Reading with God*, p. 14.

11 Robin Maas and Gabriel O' Donnell OP, *Spiritual Traditions for the Contemporary Church* (Nashville TN: Abingdon Press, 1990), p. 47.

12 Charles Dickens, *Hard Times* (1854).

13 John Pritchard, *How to Pray: A Practical Handbook* (London: SPCK, 2002), p. 48.

14 William Blake, Letter 8–9, quoted in Peter Ackroyd, *Blake* (London: Sinclair-Stevenson, 1995), p. 209.

15 Martin Luther, *A Simple Way to Pray* (1535).

16 Karl Barth, *Prayer*, 50th anniversary edn (Louisville KY: Westminster John Knox Press, 2002), p. 13.

17 Eugene Peterson, *Subversive Spirituality* (Grand Rapids MI: Eerdmans, 1997), p. 4.

18 Sharyn Echols Dowd, *Prayer, Power and the Problem of Suffering*, Dissertation Series, Society of Biblical Literature (Atlanta GA: Scholars Press, 1988), p. 2.

19 Elizabeth Struthers Malbon, *In the Company of Jesus: Characters in Mark's Gospel* (Louisville KY: Westminster John Knox Press, 2001), p. 189.

20 Morna Hooker, *The Message of Mark* (London: Epworth Press, 1983), p. 3.

21 Brueggemann, *Great Prayers of the Old Testament*, p. 76.

22 Geza Vermes, *Jesus the Jew* (London: William Collins Sons & Co., 1973), p. 200.

23 Taanit 23b in the Babylonian Talmud, quoted in Vermes *Jesus the Jew*, p. 211.

24 Barton, *The Spirituality of the Gospels*, p. 39.

25 Martin Buber, *I and Thou* (London: Continuum, 2004), p. 67.

26 Barton, *The Spirituality of the Gospels*, p. 63.

27 Ernest Best, *The Gospel as Story* (Edinburgh: T & T Clark, 1983), p. 66.

28 W. H. Vanstone, *The Stature of Waiting* (London: Darton, Longman & Todd, 1982), pp. 22–3.

29 Barton, *The Spirituality of the Gospels*, p. 63.

30 Timothy Dwyer, *The Motif of Wonder in the Gospel of Mark*, Journal of the Study of the New Testament Supplement (London: Continuum, 1996), p. 201.

31 John Donahue, 'Jesus as the Parable of God in the Gospel of Mark', *Interpretation* 32 (1978), p. 166.

32 Peterson, *Eat this Book*, p. 108.

33 J. Neville Ward, *The Use of Praying* (London: Epworth Press, 1967), p. 20.

34 Ward, *The Use of Praying*, p. 21.

35 John V. Taylor, *The Go between God: Holy Spirit and the Christian Mission* (London: SCM Press, 1975).

36 Joel Marcus, *Mark 8—16*, Anchor Bible Commentaries (New Haven CT: Yale University Press, 2009), p. 980. See also Joel Marcus, *Mark 1—8*, Anchor Bible Commentaries (New Haven CT: Yale University Press, 2007).

37 Malbon, *In the Company of Jesus*, p. 17.

38 Ched Myers, *Binding the Strong Man: A Political Reading of Mark's Story of Jesus* (Maryknoll NY: Orbis Books, 1989), p. 9.

39 Myers, *Binding the Strong Man*, p. 255.

40 Hooker, *The Message of Mark*, p. 15.

41 Iris Murdoch, *The Sovereignty of Good* (London: Routledge, 1970), p. 55.

42 Ed Sanders, *The Historical Figure of Jesus* (Harmondsworth: Penguin, 1995), p. 262.

43 Ber 32b, Babylonian Talmud, quoted in Dowd, *Prayer*, p. 349.

44 P. W. L. Walker, *Jesus and the Holy City* (Grand Rapids MI: Eerdmans, 1996), p. 11.

45 Burdon, *Stumbling on God*, p. 60.

46 Ernest Best, *Following Jesus: Discipleship in the Gospel of Mark*, Journal for the Study of the New Testament Supplement Series (Sheffield: Sheffield Academic Press, 1981), p. 243.

47 David E. Aune, *The New Testament in its Literary Environment* (Cambridge: James Clarke, 1987), p. 18.

48 Joan Mitchell, *Beyond Fear and Silence: A Feminist Reading of Mark* (London: Continuum, 2002), p. 62.

49 'The Church of Christ', from Fred Pratt Green, *26 Hymns* (London: Stainer & Bell, 1971).

50 Marcus, *Mark*, p. 220.

51 'O for a thousand tongues to sing', from Charles Wesley, *Hymns and Sacred Poems* (1740).

52 Daryl D. Schmidt, *The Gospel of Mark* (Sonomoa CA: Polebridge Press, 1991), p. 63.

53 Marcus, *Mark*, p. 291.

54 Schmidt, *The Gospel of Mark*, p. 66.

55 Charles Elliot, *Praying the Kingdom* (London: Darton, Longman & Todd, 1985), p. 88.

56 Marcus, *Mark*, p. 403.

57 Desmond Tutu, 'Goodness is stronger than evil' in Janet Morley (ed.), *Bread of Tomorrow* (London: SPCK and Christian Aid, 1992), p. 133.

58 Marcus, *Mark*, p. 426.

59 Prayer of Humble Access, Book of Common Prayer.

60 Roland Riem, *Power and Vulnerability*, Grove Series 51 (Cambridge: Grove Books, 1994), p. 5.

61 Oscar Wilde, source unknown.

62 Schmidt, *The Gospel of Mark*, p. 111.

63 Marcus, *Mark*, p. 765.

64 Frances M. Young, *Face to Face* (London: Epworth Press, 1985), p. 49.

65 Benjamin Franklin, Letter to Jean Baptiste Le Roy, 13 November 1789.

66 Marcus, *Mark*, p. 843.

67 Elizabeth Struthers Malbon, *Narrative Space and Mythic Meanings in Mark*, Biblical Seminar Series (London: Continuum, 1991), p. 164.

68 Mitchell *Beyond Fear*, p. 64.

69 C. H. Dodd, quoted in Marcus, *Mark*, p. 999.

70 Augustus Toplady, 'Rock of ages, cleft to me'.

71 Malbon, *In the Company of Jesus*, p. 11.

72 Vanstone, *The Stature of Waiting*, p. 115.

73 Best, *Mark*, p. 82.

74 Vanstone, *The Stature of Waiting*, p. 72.

75 Hooker, *The Message of Mark*, p. 119.

76 Donald Juel, *A Master of Surprise: Mark Interpreted* (Minneapolis MN: Augsburg Fortress Press, 1994), p. 120.